A Present Help ·

Marie Monsen (1878-1962)

A Present Help

Standing on the Promises of God

by Marie Monsen

Kingsley Press

Shoals, Indiana

A Present Help

PUBLISHED BY KINGSLEY PRESS
PO Box 973
Shoals, IN 47581
USA
Tel. (800) 971-7985
www.kingsleypress.com
E-mail: sales@kingsleypress.com

ISBN: 978-0-9719983-9-1

Copyright © 1960 OMF International
First printed in Great Britain 1960 by China Inland Mission
First Kingsley Press edition 2011

This first Kingsley Press edition is published under license from
OMF International, Singapore.

All Scripture, unless otherwise noted, is taken from the King James
Version of the Bible.

Printed in the United States of America.

Contents

These simple testimonies, to a faithful God who keeps His promises and never fails those He guides, are dedicated to Christian youth in conflict.

Publisher's Note

During the whole of the life and work of many missionaries in China, the incidence of lawlessness, brigandage and piracy menaced the lives and property of all who lived within its borders. The bribery and corruption of those who ruled the nation, at all levels of officialdom, caused widespread fear and poverty. Warlords lived on earnings of the unpaid soldiery, who turned to brigandage and banditry for their livelihood. Travelers by foot, litter, mule or horseback, on unmade tracks or mountain trails, or on slow river boats drawn upstream by trackers, were easy prey for innumerable marauding bands. United, these hordes of bandits could raid towns and villages, burning, killing and pillaging, or holding to ransom at will, as Miss Monsen graphically relates.

The Lord Preserveth the Strangers

Psalms 146:9

We were both newcomers and had landed in a coastal city in China within a couple of months of each other. We were to travel inland and were sent up the river by steamer to a city a few days' journey away. An English missionary was to meet us on our arrival there.

Nothing happens by chance to the children of God, nor did it to us. The steamer arrived very early one morning, three hours before it was due, so there was no one to meet us. We decided to wait on board until the missionary came, but collected all our luggage on deck—there was a good deal more than our own things to be taken into the interior. An army of coolies rushed up the gangway as soon as it was in position. Guessing that we should hardly be allowed to stay on the boat till we were called for, I walked quickly up the nearby streets to try and find someone to come to terms with the coolies. I was unsuccessful. On returning to the steamer, I saw that the men had taken matters into their own hands and were already coming down the gangway with our luggage. As I was on shore, there was nothing for it but to set out with the front carriers, while my companion brought up the rear with the last one. But where were they taking us? We could not tell them where we wanted to go, and there was a French and a German concession as well as the British one, to which they might take us. In our distress we were both praying silently while we half ran beside the men.

How far along the wide river street we had gone I do not know, when a young man suddenly dashed across the street, through the busy traffic and began gesticulating and talking to me. He ran along beside me for a while before it dawned on him that I did not understand a word of what he was saying. Then he shouted something to the coolies, who put the luggage down. He was carrying a sack on his back. He threw it down on the street, squatted beside it and opened it. Then I realized he was a postman. But what did he want with us? Piles of letters were laid out on the street. At last he found the one he was looking for and smiling, held it up for me to see. With delight I read the name and address of the missionary who was to have met us. The letters were pushed back into the sack; he pulled my sleeve and got the luggage-bearers going again. We turned up the next side street and were soon at our destination. When we had been helped to payoff the coolies and had been shown up to our room, tears of glad thankfulness came. It was a glorious entering in for us. The Lord had blessed our coming in as He has promised to do.

We heard later that the postman was a Christian. But how did he know about our predicament? To our understanding that has remained an unanswered question. Certainly the men had discussed where they should take us loudly enough, but from where he had been walking on the other side of the wide street he could not possibly have heard them. The traffic was noisy and, at that time of the day, there were also shouts of drivers hurrying their animals to the market-place. But where the understanding finds no explanation, faith reckons with God, and we believe that He told His child, the postman, of our need of help.

This experience was much in my mind, and when, soon afterwards, I read a word in the Bible, it was with the thought of what the Lord had done for us that made it a living word to me, one to which I often consciously pinned my faith in the future years spent in a foreign country: "The Lord preserveth the strangers."

He is a Stronghold in the Time of Trouble

It was a period of anti-foreign feeling. The heathen appeared to revel in showing their hatred and contempt whenever there was an opportunity, and those who did not share their antipathy were afraid to show friendliness.

I was sitting on a wretched, rickety donkey-cart. The atmosphere was charged with animosity; practically everyone I met gave vent to their feelings. The driver disliked having me as his passenger—that I soon realized. And the donkey was as obstinate as it could be.

Suddenly a drunken soldier accosted me. I had just seen him empty down a whole jug of wine at the last inn. "Stop, stop, stop!" he bawled, "I want to sit on that cart. I will protect the foreigner." His tone was such that everyone knew he meant the opposite, and the crowd that had gathered round him roared with laughter. The incident did not appear to be unwelcome to the driver, and he all of a sudden was in no manner of hurry. Fear came flooding over me.

Then I remembered how many times the words "Fear not" occur in the Bible, and the remembrance was enough to set me free from feeling afraid. The soldier came running up in drunken haste shouting, "Stop!" The driver obeyed. "Lord, Thou art 'a stronghold in the time of trouble.' I need Thy protection now. Thou art a wall of fire round about me now. I thank Thee, Lord."

The soldier put his foot on the cart, intending to climb up from the back, but he noticed that one of his ankle bands was undone. He sat down on the roadside to fasten it, and at my order the driver went on, strangely enough. The donkey got up to speed too—for the first time in the whole journey. At the next inn the soldier emptied down another jug of wine, and for some time I expected to have trouble from him. Then, in a flash, I was reminded of how a whole army was once smitten with blindness (2 Kings 6) and remembering the story, I prayed: "Lord, cause him not to see me."

From that moment it was as though he saw neither me nor the cart again, although we traveled together for quite a long way—we, down in the deep hollow which the road had become in the course of the years, he, up on the narrow footpath along the ridge above the road. He met very heavily laden barrows, their owners laboring beneath the loads, and each time he made wild attacks on them and overturned them one after another into the hollow track behind us. The same fate was dealt out to the carriers of some valuable loads of glassware. The glass trumpets were probably all smashed.

After each crazy deed the soldier came running up behind us. He seemed to like our company, but he never addressed us once. Finally he turned off at a deserted side road and we saw him no more.

"The angel of the Lord encampeth round about them that fear him, and delivereth them" (Psalms 34:7).

The Lord is Thy Keeper

Psalms 121:5

My first term in China had been struggled through. It had often been wearisome work because of illnesses due to climatic conditions. Now I was going home to Norway. My colleagues hardly realized how run down I was, but they understood enough to insist that I should have someone with me as far as the railway, which was three or four days' journey away. The choice fell on a heathen neighbor. He had often heard God's Word and was useful to us as a carrier.

The first day all went well and we spent the night with missionaries in a neighboring station. The next day, towards afternoon, I noticed three men who kept close to our cart. Now and again they chatted to the driver and told him, among other things, that there was a better road to the north-east. The driver said nothing to this.

One of the three men happened to bend down to pick up something on the road, and I saw the outline of a large knife which he was carrying under his shirt on his back. Soon afterwards I noticed the same thing about the other two. They made repeated but unsuccessful attempts to get the driver away from the main road. The word about the Lord being our keeper, quoted above, was my refuge and my prayers went up to Him.

We reached the home of some English missionaries that evening and I told them about the three men. The missionary went to the local authorities and gave them an account of the men and their description. They took it for granted that they were the three bandits they had been hunting for a long time. Next day, we were provided with an escort of six armed soldiers, but we realized that should the opportunity to share the loot arise, they would probably not be entirely reliable. The large trunk on the back of the cart must have been a continual temptation, but the journey went well.

The rest of the story I learned from a letter from the missionaries we had stayed with. The three men were all caught and they were the bandits they had been looking for. Why did they not rob me that day, when they kept so near to our cart? The big trunk was surely attractive booty and there was not very much traffic on the road. As far as I was concerned, the answer was: "The Lord is my keeper." He has at His command "angels. . . mighty in strength," which are "sent forth to do service for the sake of them that shall inherit salvation" (Hebrews 1: 14 RV).

There were a few rather tense hours after I discovered those knives. I was given help and was kept, but I am sorry to say that there was not the rest of faith within while it was happening.

That was my first meeting with brigands.

As Thy Days, So Shall Thy Strength Be

Deuteronomy 33:25

There had been times of bitter persecution just before my arrival in China and we heard and read a great deal about the sufferings of the martyrs. The result of this reading was that I became fully convinced, that if a Boxer Rebellion should happen again, there would be nothing of the stuff of martyrs in me. In the end the thought of a possible repetition of those sufferings became a nightmare to me, and I began to pray sincerely and earnestly: "O Lord, take the call away from me and send me home."

One night I dreamt that we were experiencing persecution again. We were expecting the enemies of the foreigners to be upon us any moment. There they were, shouting and looting the mission compound. I jumped out of bed. Although unseen myself, I could see their faces wild with hate and lust for blood. Strangely enough, above the din and uproar I could hear the gate-keeper's voice. He was blocking the door into the house and trying to make terms with them. He suggested that only one foreigner should be given up to them and they agreed. By this time I was dressed and it was perfectly clear that I, who was a single woman, should be the one to be given into their hands. After locking the missionary and his wife and two children into their room, I ran down the stairs, opened the door and called out: "I am the one." I was filled with peace and knew no fear.

With wild howls a horde of arms were stretched out to snatch me. I was lifted up and carried in a sitting posture so that I could see over their heads. The way led out through the city gate and along the road towards the execution ground, where they meant to feast on the foreigner. Out there in the street I was filled with abundant peace and joy. Then I awoke and quite distinctly heard the words: "As thy days, so shall thy strength be" (the Norwegian version reads:

"Thy rest shall be as long as thy days") and I sighed that it was only a dream. But the dream had a mighty influence, for from that moment I was set free from fear of death at the hands of brutal heathen men.

A Glorious Deliverance

A message came from an out-station to say that they were able to gather a group of women for a Bible course which they had been hoping to hold there for a long time. Could I come? Conditions had been unsettled for some time, but I was given a good word to travel on: "The angel of the Lord encampeth round about them that fear him and delivereth them" (Psalms 34:7).

The gate-keeper went out to hire a cart for the journey, but he could not find one. Embarrassed and stammering he stood before me: "It is still unsafe to travel. There are brigands about, so no carters are willing to go north." He saw I was disappointed and added in a fatherly tone: "It is best for you yourself not to go. Don't travel just now."

I had looked forward to the trip and now the way was closed. But not the way upward: "Lord, if this journey is Thy will, Thou canst find a cart for me." Having committed the matter to God I was at rest.

Within an hour the gate-keeper came back: "There is a cart from the north here that is going back home; the driver is here to ask if there is anyone wanting to travel north."

"Yes, I will go."

The gate-keeper looked at me despairingly, so I had to tell him of my prayer, and he answered in a very subdued voice, "Yes, this must be the answer."

The journey went well. The city gate was closed when we reached it, but it was quickly opened to such an old friend as I was.

Contrary to custom the women had arrived before me, but there was a natural explanation. There had been a great deal of unrest for a long time in the district from which they came and continual brigand attacks. At dusk they had to find hiding places in caves and among rocks and had spent whole nights in tense expectancy with very little sleep. So when they heard there was to be a Bible course in the nearest city, they did not wait long before setting out and there were many who wanted to attend. It was going to be wonderful to sleep inside the high city wall with no brigands to fear.

They were worn out after the anxious time with sleepless nights at home and slept a practically unbroken sleep through two nights and a day before we could begin the Bible course. Not one of them except the Bible-woman was saved, but they were good listeners and very willing to learn as we told them the Good News.

Just a few days later, when we were well into our course, a terrible message reached us. A large group of bandits had suddenly appeared and surrounded the city; the soldiers who ought to have been defending it were chasing bandits in quite another direction. Confusion reigned in the city. Everyone seemed to be running about thinking it would be safer to hide in someone else's house.

I shall never forget the horror that laid hold on the women in the Bible course when this news came. They felt like rats in a trap. At home they could have run away and found a place to hide in. They fell down just where they were, like lifeless bundles, and had to be helped up one by one and brought into the classroom. The hall was filling with women (and men) who knew us a little and were seeking refuge with us. They all sat there terrified and despairing. They were expecting the worst, for in a city without soldiers the bandits could harry at will. They would soon be in the city, and then?

The meeting that began then, lasted for about five hours for me, and for the others all night. The terrified people were told Bible stories of how the living God had intervened in times of trouble. They heard of Daniel and his friends, of Jeremiah and Jonah and all the others who experienced deliverance. The promises of God were repeated over and over again until they remembered them. Then we prayed. True, they did not know how to pray, but from full hearts they joined in saying over the petitions they heard being made. They received the Word as little children do.

Late in the evening I could not keep up any longer and went and lay down fully dressed. The last sounds I heard from the people in the hall were: "The Lord is a wall of fire round about His people," and "His loving kindness is new every morning," and "Thou shalt not be afraid of the terror by night." Then I fell asleep.

When day dawned I was awakened by the women rushing into my room, each shouting to drown the rest: "We are saved," "We are delivered," "God has great power," "Nothing is difficult to Him," "Not a shot has been fired here tonight," "And now the bandits are leaving the city."

The men had already run out and gone up on to the city wall to see with their own eyes that the bandits were going away. They came back and said: "None of those we talked to can understand why the bandits are leaving the city without firing a single shot. They must know through their spies that there are no soldiers here. There are the marks of two cannons outside the city wall."

Some of our friends went out later and saw those marks.

But the group that had been gathered in our hall that night understood that the living God had delivered us from danger. How happy they were! It was the first time they had experienced the power of the God we told them of, and now they were keener than ever to learn.

Not many days later this happened:

The door of the classroom was pushed open by two men, carrying a very sick woman between them. They looked in amazement at the unusual sight of so many women gathered together and asked hesitatingly:

"Isn't it here Jesus lives?"

"Yes," the women answered in unison.

Someone jumped up and fetched a straw mat to lay on the earthen floor, so that the sick woman could lie down.

"I want to ask if Jesus can heal my wife."

"Yes, He can," the crowd of simple women answered in chorus.

"She has been ill a long time, and hasn't been able to eat for a long time either." (When a person could not eat, he was accounted very ill indeed).

"Have you any idols at home?" the Bible-woman asked.

Yes, he had.

"How many?"

He went over their names.

"Well, you see," the Bible-woman replied, "Jesus and idols don't go together. Will you take down your idols and bring them here to burn?"

"Yes, if only my wife will get well, I will," and he ran home for his idols. They were counted and burned.

The women knelt all round the sick woman and prayed for her in a great choir of prayer. No one looked at me. I sat in the same seat all the time, a very interested onlooker. After a while the Bible-woman said:

"Now you can stop praying. You remember Jesus said that they should make some food for Jairus' daughter?"

Yes, they remembered.

"Now some of you must make some food for this woman, you heard her husband say she hadn't eaten anything for a long time."

Several ran away, the rest sat round the sick woman while the Bible-woman talked to her. They all assented eagerly to everything she said.

Then the food was brought, a large, deep dish brimming over. Their idea was, evidently, that there should be plenty for a person who had not eaten for a long time. It was enough for a laborer, made of the roughest, blackest cereal. I was just going to rise and prevent them from giving it to her, as it was not food for a sick woman; but the Bible woman stopped me from interfering when she said:

"It will be impossible for you to eat this food unless we first ask God to bless it."

They did so.

"And now you can eat. The food God has blessed cannot harm you."

The woman ate, sitting there on the mat.

"That's right, now we will help you up so that you can sit on a bench until we have finished our lesson."

She stayed for two lessons, then she went home alone and cooked the dinner for her family and came back to the afternoon class.

Many came later to hear the Word because of this woman's testimony.

I Will Not Destroy it for the Ten's Sake

Genesis 18:32

As usual it came suddenly. A notorious band of brigands was on its way towards the city, and the people were fleeing in hot haste. Even people from the suburb in which I was leading a study course for Bible-women were fleeing. The confusion was indescribable. Many even ran away from their old folk leaving them to "keep the gate." The Bible-women had gathered from two provinces, and only a few of them knew the district. They were told immediately that they were quite free to leave, and that although I myself felt perfectly assured that I was to stay where I was, none of them were to remain on that account. We had a time of prayer together and at the close those who wished to flee were advised to go immediately, but they all chose to stay where they were. We decided to spend a while in private prayer alone, and without speaking to others to ask God to give each of us a word from the Bible to rest upon.

When we met again, they were asked one by one what word had been given. After the first two had answered, they all brightened up noticeably. I began to guess what was coming: they had all been given the same word. I might have doubted that it was really so but for the overwhelming realization that I myself had been given the very same promise: "I will not destroy it (the city) for the ten's sake" (Genesis 18:32 RV).

"And we are more than ten here," the women said joyfully.

The text was not one we had read together in our Bible course either. We had a good time of praise together. All the anxiety for the group of women I was responsible for had blown away so to speak.

We lay down in our clothes that night. There was some shooting and some heavy bombing too at first, then all was silent. Early in the morning we were told that the bandits had left the city in great haste. They were said to have heard that a large army was coming to relieve the city and was not far off. We were a very happy group of women that day. We had personally experienced the presence of God, for one of His own promises had been literally fulfilled before our eyes.

No relieving army ever arrived.

With God All Things Are Possible

Matthew 19:26

We had spent a splendid week up in the mountain district among a group of believers. We had even been able to hold meetings for their heathen neighbors and relatives. On account of the brigand bands it had not been possible to visit this group for a long time. When things were quieter and they could breathe freely at last, they had asked for a week's meetings. It was good to see them again and hear more of the troubles they had lived through and of the help from God they had experienced in the midst of it all.

We parted glad and thankful over the days together. But they were strangely loud-voiced in their joy and I could not quite understand why. Later I was told that they had all kept silent about a thing the leaders had sternly forbidden them to tell me. I was not to be told till I was out of the district and across the river. That was the only time in over twenty years that I found Chinese who could keep a secret.

It was strange and unusual too, that four of the leaders insisted on escorting me "out of the district and across the river." When we were on the other side they explained the "something" I had felt the last day or two among them.

In the middle of the week they had been informed by an express messenger that the brigands who usually camped in the nearby mountains, and who they thought were operating in other parts, had unexpectedly come home. They were just going to set out again which meant they would pass through the neighborhood that evening or in the night.

The leaders had consulted together and agreed that nothing was to be said to me. The sons of some of the Christians were sent to meet the believers on their way home after the last meeting of the day to tell them about the situation, and to ask them to pray especially for me. The brigands always halted in that valley when they passed through it, and their chief usually occupied the room I was living in. It was in the best house in the place. The four leaders had agreed to stand on guard outside my door, and to risk all to prevent anyone entering.

The brigand army came, but contrary to their custom they did not halt in the valley that night. They rushed at full speed through the valley, probably to make a lightning raid somewhere else. My sleep was usually "sweet" (Proverbs 3:24), but that night it must have been extra sweet and deep, since I did not hear the crowd of mounted brigands dashing past the wall of the room in which I was sleeping.

As they told it, I suddenly recalled how one day many of the friends had asked me how I had slept and how they smiled and nodded to each other. The heavy sleep was God's answer to their prayers for me.

Why had they not told me and moved me to another house? They explained, that unused as I was to their troubled conditions, they thought I would have been afraid and would have gone home. They could not bear to think that they might miss a single day of the week that had been promised them, and besides, they could turn to God about it all.

It was a wonderful praise meeting we had by the riverside, one of the sacred hours of my life on the mission field. I stood there, looking at those four sons of the mountains, once heathen, but kept from becoming brigands, now, willing to give their lives for one of the messengers of the Gospel who had come among them. They had solemnly pledged together that none of them would fail me.

"Other fell into the good ground, and grew, and brought forth fruit a hundredfold" (Luke 8:8 RV).

A Later Visit to the Same Neighborhood

It had again been impossible to visit that group up in the north for several years, when one day an express messenger came to ask for at least a short visit, if only for one day.

The day they had chosen themselves was a Sunday. It meant leaving at once if I was to reach them. The first day's journey was by cart, and by making a very early start the next morning, Sunday, I could be with them in time for the morning service. This was probably what the friends had intended.

As I sat thinking that Saturday evening of meeting the group the next day, the evangelist at the out-station at which I was to spend the night, came in and told me that there was unrest in the northern district again and I ought not to go. While I stood thinking it over, it began to pour with rain. The evangelist said that if it went on raining like that all night, I could not reach my destination before midday, and then I would only just be able to meet the friends and turn round and come back at once. My prayer then was, that if the Lord wanted me to go the next morning, the rain might soon stop. It was dark and cloudy, but it soon stopped raining, and it did not rain any more that night. That settled the matter for me.

It was with inward joy and peace that I set out. The day was perfect and the road free from dust. The driver had only promised to see me across the river, and there was no bridge. When we reached the opposite bank, an evangelist came to meet me with a message from the group in the mountains to say that there was trouble again, and perhaps it was best I should not go any further. Their messenger had picked his way over a rocky pass because he did not dare to walk along the ordinary road.

"But you can't walk through those rocks," he said, "so there is no way through for you today." It came very conclusively.

I stood still a few minutes. The evangelist had told me that the chapel would be full for the morning service. The rain had stopped, and that was the sign I had asked that I should carry the journey through. Yes, I must go on, and I felt deep peace in the decision. I knew it was God's will for me.

"If you go by the road through the valley, I will go with you," the evangelist said. On his advice, the muleteer went back across the river where he was to wait for me till he saw me coming back. There was no traffic on the road. We passed a village which lay deserted and silent as though its inhabitants were all dead. Not even a hen clucked. The people were, of course, hiding far up among the rocks, and since they had not come back although it was broad day, the bandits must have been at no great distance.

"The angel of the Lord encampeth round about them that fear him, and delivereth them," I repeated to myself as we walked, and I thanked God for that word.

There was great joy among all those who had gathered for the meeting from all over the valley. Scouts, who had been on the lookout, reported that four bandits were hiding in the silent village through which we had passed. We guessed they were sleeping after a busy night.

It was a hearty, happy reunion and we had two profitable gatherings round the promises of God. In the dinner hour they listened to news of other stations and I heard a little of their trials and of how God had cared for them.

We broke up early. The evangelist went with me, and the whole group continued in prayer until their scouts reported that I was safely across the river and had been fetched by the muleteer.

Once again I had walked within the shelter of the wall of fire. I was clearly led back by the same road I had come, and the village was not quite as deserted as it had been earlier in the day. Later I heard that a heathen man said an hour after I had passed through the village: "If the foreigner can walk through there and get safely across the river, I can too." He was taken by the bandits who were still in the village.

The Peace of God Which Passeth Understanding

When the following happened, I was the only missionary on the station. Before I went upstairs to bed, I shut all the windows of the house as usual and locked the two doors.

I was awakened in the night by two heavy blows on my right shoulder and was terrified. Robbers, was my first thought. Then the words sounded clearly and distinctly: *"The Lord is a wall of fire round about His people."* Immediately fear gave place to quiet, strengthening joy over this wonderful truth. And then the Lord allowed me to see it. It was as if the roof had been lifted off the house, and sitting up in bed I was surrounded by a very high wall of fire. It gave out no heat. A swarm of arrows came flying from beyond the wall, but not one of them reached me. The vision lasted perhaps only a second or two.

I found myself sitting with tears of joy streaming down my face: "Is it *like that,* Lord, Thou art round about Thy people, and I have never known it before."

Then, very naturally the question arose: "Why should I have this experience now?" It was peaceful in the city and its environs, and as far as I knew no other danger threatened.

In the forenoon of the following day a messenger arrived from the nearest mission station with the request that I should come and join with them in prayer for the missionaries' little son, who had suddenly become seriously ill. The message had taken a long time to reach me. The bearer had only been able to travel in daylight because of brigands infesting the roads. I prepared to set out at once. In spite of very bad weather I was able to procure a cart and left about midday.

The driver I had that day was not one I would have chosen. I had had him before, and he usually gave vent to a continuous stream of curses all day. He was a heathen man and it seemed as though everything I said to him simply glanced aside.

We were hardly outside the city gate before I noticed that the peace of God seemed to fill the atmosphere round me; even the landscape seemed full of the peace of God. In the cart it felt like a soft warmth wrapped round me. I have no words with which to describe it. The driver felt it too, to such an extent that he never uttered a curse all day, although the roads were very bad. In several places the cart slid slowly through the mud without the wheels going round. The whip, which was usually applied to the animals when they were struggling hardest, was not used that day at all. It was all so wonderful that I thought more than once: "Will it be like this in the Millennium?"

At six in the evening it grew dark. We had reached a small village where the animals were to be fed, but we had another seven miles to go. While we waited there, a soldier came over to speak to me. He appeared to know who I was and asked if I intended to go on in the dark. When I answered that we meant to do so, he warned me earnestly against going on that evening. Out on the slopes along the road we were to travel, it was swarming with robbers after dark. Scores of people had simply disappeared there within the past month. He finished by saying: "I don't dare to go any further tonight."

The vision of the previous night came vividly to mind. I had nothing to fear. And the more than amazing thing was that the driver, who had been standing listening to all the soldier said, made no objection at all to going on. We could neither buy nor borrow a lantern.

"For that matter we couldn't use a lantern," the driver remarked. He managed to procure several boxes of matches. He often had to strike a match to see whether we were on the road or not.

I sat in the cart, safe, happy and peaceful, thrilling with the certainty that not even an army a thousand strong could harm me that evening, because of the wall of fire round about me. All who have lived in China know that it was most unusual to travel seven miles in the dark without even hearing a dog bark. There must have been a higher power guiding the driver and holding the reins that evening—He who is a wall of fire round about His people. I had often read about the wall of fire and known of it earlier, but that night I believed in it as never before.

It was strange to be sitting there under those circumstances, feeling as quiet and safe as I do while I sit writing about it today. I began to realize a little how wide is the scope of the promise: "My peace I give unto you," and how much the words in 1 John 5:4 mean, "This is the victory that overcometh the world, even our faith" (faith that has been given to us by God).

Those who had been looking out for us at the city gate had given us up long before we reached it, but the gate was opened to us, as the keeper knew we were expected. The little boy was better. The prayer that had been sent up both from the mission station and the cart on the road had already been answered.

After that, the wall of fire was a grand, blessed reality which I reckoned with by faith countless times in my missionary life in China; but this experience was the beginning of my conscious faith in it.

Lo, I Am With You Always, Even Unto the End of the World

Matthew 28:20

A course for Bible-women was to be held in Tengchow. The first part of the road, about twenty miles, was dangerous traveling on account of robbers. Some of the women had already come as far as our station, Nanyang, and others were due to join us on the way. It was no small responsibility to travel with this group of women on perilous roads. They wrote from Tengchow to say that the last twenty miles were not safe either. Yet it was not easy to postpone the course, as several women were already on their way from other stations.

It had not been made clear to me what we were to do, when the post came. In a letter to me, someone had sent a little hand-painted card with the words of the text quoted above. It was just as though the Lord's voice spoke to me through that word, and in a moment the whole problem was solved, "I—Jesus—am with you all the days." That was enough to travel on. The decision brought peace of heart. The seven women who were to go with me were told about the text that had been given for the journey, but they were also given full liberty to stay behind if they wished. They all came with me.

We left that same day. As our own mission cart and driver were going, we succeeded in hiring a second cart in spite of the troubled conditions. We got safely through the first ten miles and spent the night at an out-station. Next morning, I felt constrained to make an early start. The drivers did not agree with me about this, but when I told them that I believed an early start was going to mean something special to us that day, they gave in.

We would not delay for breakfast; we could have it later at an inn on the road. When we got there we would be halfway to our destination, and the worst part of the journey would be behind us.

While the women were enjoying their warm breakfast gruel at our first halt, our own driver came and asked to speak to me outside.

"Look," he said, "other carters have turned round and are whipping their animals like madmen to go back as fast as they can; we had better do the same. Part of a brigand army has just come, and they are having breakfast at the inn outside the south gate."

We were outside the east gate of the little town, but the corner of the town wall prevented us from seeing them. The "bridge" across the trench which ran along the town wall had been taken away, and only a plank had been left. The civil defense had quickly gathered on the wall, armed with sticks, spades, pitchforks and stones.

"I am with you all the days." I asked the driver to run and enquire whether they would allow us to drive through the town. He soon returned with a blank refusal. All at once I saw the solution of the problem. The brigands had just arrived, worn, weary and hungry after the exploits of the night. They would take plenty of time over their meal. The road we were going to travel by would be hidden from their view by the town wall.

With this in my mind, I walked across the narrow plank to the gate and explained my plan to the gatekeeper and one or two others on the inside. They could see me through a crack in the gate, and recognized me from many visits in the course of the years. The permission was given and planks were laid across the trench. The second driver followed ours without a protest, and, at a speed I had never before experienced in China, we drove through the town without being seen by the bandits. We were soon over the ridge outside the walls of the town, and how thankful we were!

We met people on the road who were acting as scouts, taking note of the lay of the land. They informed us of unrest in one place and another. There were no other carts to be seen. We reached our goal safely. The promise given us for our journey did not fail. It was an enriching experience to us all.

Another Journey By the Same Road

Once again it was a trip for the same purpose with a group of Bible-women going to the annual Bible course. The times were troubled, but there was a good deal of traffic on the road, so we were not expecting any special incidents. Once again we had two carts, our own and a hired one. After dinner, which we had eaten at an outstation, we were to cross a river. On account of heavy rains, the water was so deep that carts had to wait their turn to cross at the right place.

While we were waiting, a sergeant came up to the cart on which I was sitting and requisitioned it for himself and a soldier. We could have his cart instead, a little donkey cart, which could never keep up with the vehicle we had hired. He was not sober, and felt it was beneath his dignity as an officer that others should have better animals and a better cart than he.

I was quite calm. The carts, the animals and the women were all in the Lord's service, we could safely leave ourselves in His care. I informed the sergeant that he could not have the cart, since the General himself had given us a safe-conduct for it—for the first time, as a matter of fact. We who were on the cart remained quietly where we were in spite of all his threatenings and the play-acting he went through with his rifle. Suddenly the driver saw it was our turn to cross the river and set off with a jerk, followed by the second cart. The sergeant, who had been holding on, had perforce to let go. Probably he was so drunk that he never thought of hauling himself up on to our cart. The donkey-cart brought up the rear with the roaring, swearing sergeant. He probably felt that he had "lost face" in the eyes of all the other travelers. As soon as his donkey cart was across the ford, he ran ahead of it and caught up with us in a narrow little pass before we reached the level.

The soldier came up too and they stopped our animals. Then they came back to us in the cart. The driver was holding the reins, but he could not pass the officer who was trying to drag me down, while the soldier laid hold on an elderly Bible-woman. We two were sitting at the front of the cart to shelter the younger women who were sitting inside. The Bible-woman immediately jumped down and hung on to the soldier's rifle, so that he could not obey an order to shoot. She was given supernatural strength to hold on, she said later, and she used her time well, talking sense to the soldier, telling him how idiotic it was to take such orders from a drunken officer.

I sat still, looking into the face of the officer which was white with rage.

"You know you and your family will get the worst of this if an accident happens. You see that I am not afraid of you, and I am not afraid to be shot either."

At that he let go of me and began to attack the driver. I jumped down and stood between the two of them.

"The driver is our servant and the safe-conduct applies to him too. The General has signed it himself, so you will have him to reckon with on the driver's account as much as on ours.

Meanwhile the Bible-woman had brought the soldier to his senses. He realized that the many onlookers who had gathered were vociferously on our side. Most of them had some bone or other to pick with the military, it appeared, and the situation gave them courage to express their opinions freely. The soldier managed to check the officer's aggression. The Bible-woman had been calling upon Him, who alone could deliver us in our predicament, and He kept His promise: "Call upon me in the day of trouble: I will deliver thee, and thou shalt glorify me." We praised and glorified Him together.

We were to spend the night at one of our out-stations. I told the evangelist what had been in my mind the remaining part of the journey. He agreed with me, and we went together to the local authorities and told them about the episode. We said that we did not wish the officer to be punished, but that he ought to be reprimanded, so that other travelers need not be exposed to similar indignities. They promised to see to the matter, and they kept their word.

The officer was thoroughly punished notwithstanding. The evangelist told us later that when the sergeant and the soldier were called up to answer for their behavior, they were not only given a reprimand, but what was worse, they were led out and mocked by their colleagues because they had attempted to fight a group of women and had been beaten. It was not likely that they could continue a military career in those parts, as they would never be able to get away from such a story.

Angel Guardians

It was at an out-station. We were almost at the end of some Bible classes. Early one morning there was a fever of unrest everywhere because of rumors that there was a revolt among the soldiers in the city where we had our main station. If anything should happen, I knew I ought to be there, as the missionary in residence had a weak heart, his wife was expecting an addition to the family very soon and the nurse who had come to help her had bad nerves.

At last I succeeded in getting a donkey-cart. We crawled along for about ten miles and were the last to squeeze in through the city gate as it was being shut for the night.

When I reached home, I heard from one who knew some of the soldiers, that the General, who had no money, had promised them that one night they could loot the city instead of receiving their pay. It was expected to happen that night. A couple of soldiers had called at our mission compound in the morning to calculate how many rifles they would need to use there for the night's work. Someone had heard them say that they could manage it with eighteen rifles. Some claimed that they had heard from reliable sources that the looting was to begin at 10 o'clock when a fire was to be lit in a particular house in the center of the city quite near us. No fire was lit there, however, but in many other parts of the city. The soldiers were too impatient to wait for the signal, and began looting at 8 o'clock. We heard shooting and noise all night, until towards morning it grew quiet.

No soldiers visited us, but many of our neighbors in fear and distress came climbing over the walls round our mission compound, each carrying a little bundle of valuables.

As I was physically the most fit, I had to take charge of all these neighbors and see them comfortably installed. When we ran across the open courtyard, bullets whistled above our heads, and I realized that it was for this particular piece of work I had had to come home. The whole time the lovely old words kept sounding in my heart: "Thou shalt not be afraid for the terror by night, nor for the arrow that flieth by day," Psalms 91:5, and I added on my own account: "Nor for the bullets that have replaced arrows."

The Chinese Christians on our mission compound immediately testified boldly to the terrified heathen who had taken refuge with us. The Christians scattered naturally among them, so that there were a few of them in each room, and they truly made the most of this unusual opportunity. The heathen saw some of their own people who were quite different from themselves, without the fear they felt. We heard the noise outside all the time, but no butt-end of a gun battered at any of our four gates.

Next day, several of our neighbors across the street came in to see us. There were no walls round the houses on their side of the street, and they asked if they might knock at our gate and come in and stay with us next time there was trouble, "For you have protection," they said. I heard that remark several times before I realized that they must mean something special by the protection they spoke of. What they told me sent me calling on all the neighbors in the houses across the street, so as to hear it from several eye-witnesses.

All our neighbors had kept their doors locked that night until they were forced to open them by the roars of the soldiers and their thundering knocks. But now and again they had opened their doors to peep out and see if there was a fire anywhere near. That was when they had seen our "protectors." Three soldiers stood on guard up on the high roof of the Gospel Hall, one at each end and one in the middle. A fourth had been seated on the porch over the main gate. These soldiers had kept watch in every direction.

"Who did you think it was?"

"Soldiers the General had sent to protect you."

"Did they look like the General's soldiers?"

"They were taller than any soldiers we had seen."

"Were they armed?"

"We didn't see that, we only saw their silhouettes, we didn't dare take time to look at them carefully."

"Could you see their faces?"

"We saw them best of all."

"How was that?"

"They shone."

"Who were they like?"

"They were foreigners." (i.e. not Chinese.)

Later in the day a Christian woman brought in a heathen man. She was bursting to speak and dancing from one foot to the other in her eagerness. She said to the man:

"Now, you can ask yourself."

"Who were standing out on the east verandah all last night?"

"There was no one there. I locked the door to the verandah myself and all who were in the house were downstairs."

"No, there were many people there each time I opened my door to see if there was a fire anywhere near us. I couldn't understand it, because everyone else wanted to be under cover on such a night."

"It must have been angels on guard."

"There, listen to that," the woman said, "now you have heard it yourself, that is just what I said too."

The heathen saw them, it was a testimony to them, but they were invisible to us. It came powerfully to me and showed me how little we reckon with "The Lord, the God of hosts," who sends forth His angels, mighty in strength, "to do service for the sake of them that shall inherit salvation" (Hebrews 1:14 RV).

From that time, Psalms 84:12 was a word I learned to abide in consciously by faith for the rest of my time in China: "O Lord of hosts, blessed is the man that trusteth in thee."

This special protection was given for the sake of the three who were so unfit just then to face the grim things happening in the city; and the rest of us on the compound were included in it.

His Truth Is a Shield and a Buckler

Psalms 91:4

The holidays were over. Missionaries were leaving the mountain health resorts to return to their work, I to a course for Bible-women. Torrential rains had made the shorter route across the mountains impassable and the longer way—down one river and up another—was robber infested. Way or no way, however, I was definitely guided to go and to take the longer route. "He that keepeth Israel" were the words ringing in my heart.

A younger missionary was to help with the teaching in the Bible course and was told that I felt assured I should go.

"If you go, I go," was her immediate response.

"That is not sufficient reason for your going."

Next day she came back.

"I'm going, but not because you are going this time."

Other missionaries, a married couple and two Norwegian-American women missionaries joined us, trusting in the Lord who was able to keep us through the dangers by the way until we all reached our stations.

On the journey up river, we had to travel in small boats, which would not be too heavy to tow upstream. The current was very strong after all the rain. This meant we had three boats with two of us in each and our luggage.

When we had swung out into the river up which we were to travel, we met a crowd of soldiers coming downstream. They hailed us and said that we ought not to go any further until they came back and could be our escort.

"If we had nothing better to trust in, it would not be a pleasant situation," the man of our party remarked.

Each evening, when the boats had tied up for the night, it was delightful to get a little exercise on the bank of the river. One evening we had a long broad sandbank at our disposal and enjoyed it immensely, till the married woman of the group suddenly said: "I have a strange feeling of oppression here, what can it be?" We studied the landscape and discovered that half-hidden behind some trees up near the fields, some men were lurking. Just then one of our boatmen came running towards us and said that we must hurry on board as the place was unsafe. They had probably seen from the boats what we ourselves had just noticed. There were no other boats moored there but our three.

The boats could not move either up or downstream as it was too dark. They pushed off from the bank and anchored as far out in the river as they dared. We spent the time in prayer. The boatmen said that the rain would drive the robber's home, "because lice breed too fast in weather like this."

We had a quiet night. Next morning, one of the Norwegian-American ladies said that just before she fell asleep, the thought occurred to her that their boat with a good deal of mission money on board was moored nearest the river-bank; but she had smiled at her own thought, when she remembered that it was the Lord we were trusting to take care of our boats, so it did not matter which one was nearest the water's edge. On that she went to sleep. Very thankfully we continued our journey the next morning.

Another day, we reached a place early in the forenoon where there were several rafts, each consisting of a large number of small boats. Those traveling in them were afraid to go on up the river, because there were robbers a short way ahead behind a promontory which we could see jutting out into the water. The captain of our boat told us this.

"What shall we do?" he asked.

"We can only go on. You know, we told you we have the angels of God watching over us."

He nodded.

"If you say we are to go on, we'll go on."

With that he felt no more responsibility. It was a miracle that he was willing. How much had he and the other boatmen grasped of what we had told them each evening?

We went on then, to the great amazement of all the people on the boats moored on the other side of the river,

At the tip of the promontory in front of us stood an armed sentinel, posted there by the robber band. When he saw us coming, he ran away, probably to report that three boats were approaching. Our boat rounded the point, the other two had dropped some way behind; perhaps the boatmen had agreed that this was the safest mode of procedure. Above the promontory we had to tack across the river, and prepared to do so. The captain pulled up two planks from the deck and gave us each one. We were to help them to row, using these planks as oars, as the boatmen were needed for other work. Unpracticed as we were in the art of rowing with such heavy oars against a rapid current, what little we did was of small use. Merely holding on to the oars so as not to lose them in the swift stream was rather too much for our strength. Suddenly we realized that the boat had turned round and was going back downstream.

"What are you doing?"

"Didn't you see? Didn't you hear?"

"No."

"One of the robbers came down to the edge of the river and called us back. I daren't do anything but turn round; he said he would shoot if we didn't come back."

We caught sight of him just as he lowered his rifle. He was standing staring. Suddenly he began to run more swiftly than either of us had ever seen a Chinese run before. Had he seen the angel watchers we knew were there? We never heard, but what happened later on this journey gave us cause to think so.

Now we were on the robbers' side of the river again with the two other boats quite a long way behind us. They had seen our maneuver and wondered what it meant; they could not see the robbers from where they were.

Our captain thought that those in the other boats should be told of the situation.

"Yes, run back and tell them"; he was barefoot and used to the muddy river-bank, was my thought.

"No, you are the captain of the boat on this journey, so you must go." He was obviously afraid.

"Yes, I'll go, you know I trust in the wall of fire and the angels."

I knew full well that the robbers would keep me in view every step of the way, but I trusted in God's presence, and He let me feel His nearness. A marvelous, God-given zest in conflict came, as I put my trust in God as a wall of fire between the robbers and me. Never before had I walked along any path with such conscious joy of heart.

When I reached the boats which were lying still, waiting, I explained the situation to those on board and we agreed to keep together. They could not travel down the river then, anyway. I went back in one of the two boats, and could not but admire the boatmen who were risking their boats and their very lives for our sakes. This too was the Lord's doing, since He had led us to choose this route.

To our amazement and delight, the robbers themselves did not approach our boats, but an old man who lived nearby came with a message from them to say that we might proceed up river. This confirmed us in believing that their sentinel had seen something. With thankful hearts and in great joy, we continued our journey. "The angel of the Lord encampeth round about them that fear him, and delivereth them" (Psalm 34:7). It is wonderful to have a promise like that and to have real practical faith in it in times of peril.

A little later, when I was on deck helping the boat people to punt, I noticed a number of men in the fields a little further up on the "robber side" of the river. I did not doubt it was another band of robbers. A small boat put out from the bank on our side, and came close to our boat.

"Don't you understand what sort of people they are?" and he pointed with his nose towards the men I had seen.

"Yes, they are robbers."

"Then how do you *dare* travel on?"

"We have an escort."

"I don't see it," said the old man as he peered round in every direction.

"No, you probably don't, but they are here. They are heavenly soldiers. They are in front of us and behind us and on both sides of us."

He stuck his oars straight down into the sandy riverbed and held his boat there. As long as we could see him he stood there, amazed at what must have been as incomprehensible to him as anything he had ever seen or heard.

A little further on we saw robbers on our side of the river too, on the opposite bank from where we had seen them before. They were also up in the fields; eight of them were clearly visible. One of them came down to the riverside and stood there with his gun aimed at us. I called out to my fellow-passenger inside the boat. I had been listening to her voice for some time singing in unwavering faith:

> *Strong to save, the Lord our Rock,*
> *Stands, the Rock of Ages,*
> *Guarding well His little flock,*
> *While the devil rages.*
> *Like a circling wall of fire*
> *Father-arms surround them,*
> *And no threat, however dire,*
> *Enters to confound them.*
> *Camped about God's children dear,*
> *Angel guards, unsleeping,*
> *Swift to serve and save from fear,*
> *Faithful watch are keeping.*

(The verse was improvised, woven together from the promises in Psalms 62:2, 125:2; Zechariah 2:5; Psalms 34:7.)

A hymn was sung too, slightly altered so as to bring in the perils among robbers through which we were passing.

By now we were within hailing distance, and to my own astonishment, it was I who spoke first.

"Has it rained much in these parts?"

"Yes, it has rained a good deal," came the very lame reply.

"Are the crops in danger of being spoiled?"

"We could save some if only we had good weather," he said in the same tone.

"It was a bad year last year, so it would be hard on the people here if it were a bad year again, wouldn't it?"

He nodded. I realized that the very mild tone of his voice was due to his complete amazement at being able to understand a foreigner at all. He lowered his gun and stood leaning on it.

"Who are you? Where do you come from? Where are you going? How many of you are there? Are all the three boats one party? What have you in your boats?"

His questions were answered briefly and politely, but no reference was made to the money.

"You may go on."

"Yes, God above, in whom we trust, decides that. No one can stop us if He wants us to continue our journey."

He nodded in assent as if he understood, fired a shot into the air and shouted to the robbers on the other side that no one need cross over as these boats were to continue their journey.

· · · · ·

It was a party of missionaries filled with praise and joy that met that evening, when the boats were moored for the night. We had all six been one in faith, one in spirit, with no dissonance at all, it was a benediction.

Further up the river our ways parted. The fellow-worker who was to help me at the Bible course had to go home first.

The upper reach of the river we considered less disturbed than the part we had traveled along. One evening my boat did not reach the place where river-craft usually spent the night. When there were many boats together the boatmen felt safer, and intending robbers would be exposed to a greater risk. We had to put inshore where only two other boats had stopped. The captain went ashore to ascertain the lay of the land.

"It may be all right, but you can't call it a safe place," he said. I lay down fully dressed, holding the word about the wall of fire between me and any possible "guests." As usual I had a talk with the boat people in the evening about the God who has given us the promises and always keeps His word, and about the Savior Jesus Christ whom He sent to us. There was a happy, free atmosphere between them and me and they had become very good listeners. They asked if they might spend the night in the cabin with me and I understood they were afraid.

In the night we heard shooting and shrieking as the very roughest treatment was meted out first on one boat and then on the other, then it grew quiet. We sat as silent as mice, not breathing a word until, very faintly, day began to dawn. I had been kept without fear, though there was tension, not least during the actual attack, and with all my heart I desired that the boat people might be given yet another experience of God as the living God.

When we dared to move, the captain slipped across to the other boats. They were in a fearful state and not a soul was to be seen. We were not long in getting away as quietly as possible. When we were out of sight of the place and dared to speak again, the captain kept saying "Truly, truly!" The robbers must have known there were three boats. Did they see the angels guarding us when it came to our turn to be looted? At breakfast time, when we thought it was peaceful enough, we took time to thank the Lord, the prayer of thanksgiving being punctuated all through by the captain's continual "Truly, truly!"

On arriving at our destination the boat people made a most unusual request. They wondered if we would allow them to spend a day with us, so that they could hear more.

Usually they were eager to be hired again as soon as possible.

That trip opened my eyes once more to see how often the Lord calls Himself "the Lord of hosts" in the Bible, and I thought with amazement how little we present-day believers reckon with His hosts or believe in them, although the Scripture says that they are "all ministering spirits, sent forth to do service for the sake of them that shall inherit salvation" (Hebrews 1: 14 RV).

Another Journey on the Same River

This journey took place considerably earlier than the one just described and fell out somewhat differently. I was the only passenger. For several reasons I had to travel fast as we had been lying still for some days because the current was too strong. At last a few boats began to move, among them mine, though the boat people were most reluctant. They knew what a river in spate was, and I did not.

All went well, though it was very hard work. Then we came to a bend in the river where we had to encounter the full force of the current. It was there the tow-rope snapped. The boat sped swiftly downstream; the captain's wife was the only one on board with any knowledge of navigation, for I knew nothing at all of such things. After a while we drifted towards the bank. We waited there what seemed a very long time to the impatient passenger while the rest of the crew walked back along the tow-path. After a lot of palaver—the boat people claimed more money for the journey on account of this delay—they set to work to splice the rope. They took ample time for the job. When they were ready at last, they declared that they were shorthanded and could not undertake to go on.

Fortunately, there was an out-station nearby and the evangelist there helped me to find some reliable men who could help us past the most difficult part of the river.

It was a relief to be setting out again and with sufficient crew, but when we had all but cleared the difficult stretch of water, the rope snapped again and I was almost knocked overboard when I was thrown crashing against the gunwale. We were soon back at the same place, where they had spliced the rope and from which we had started that morning.

In due course the captain came back gesticulating and cursing so violently, that the men the evangelist had found to help me fled in haste, and I had no chance even to speak a word with them.

This time there was to be no mending of the rope, there was only a ceaseless flood of oaths which drove the missionary inside and down on her knees in profound consciousness of her utter helplessness in the uneven contest with the elements, the rotten tow-rope, the cursing heathen, and my own impatient spirit and inability to adjust myself to the rhythm of Chinese life, and first and foremost there was a sense of condemnation over having fallen short in one thing—waiting on the Lord. Would it not be better that another, better fitted for the task, should take my place? Then my own failure, the whole journey, the boat, the boat people and the flooded river were all cast upon the Lord, the Master of missions and of missionaries.

While I was still kneeling in prayer the captain's wife came rushing in.

"Did you hear that?"

"No, what?"

"I heard you praying to your God. You prayed for help, didn't you? Your God is truly God, only you ought to have asked for help before. They have just called to us from that nearest group of boats and asked if they could join us. They have a mast to pull on and good tow-ropes, but not enough crew. Here they come!" And she dashed out.

The help was more than welcome. It was overwhelming grace towards one who felt she was a complete failure and was on the verge of despair, and who, moreover, had just been given smarting correction by a heathen woman. To this spiritual pauper the Lord bowed down and said: "Before you call, I will answer." Truly, He is the God of all grace.

I thanked God later, when He allowed me to travel up that river again with faith and confidence in Him, as I related in the last section.

The Time the Bandit Missed

Two of us were traveling together to a city and district which had an especially bad reputation for bandits. We were looking forward to meeting the group of Christians up there while things were fairly peaceful. There were plenty of traces of the bandits' doings—burned-out houses, deserted farms, little heaps of bones lying here and there by the roadside.

We spent a good week with the Christians and the time went all too quickly. The journey back was delightful in beautiful weather and we enjoyed the fresh mountain air. Even the donkeys seemed to catch the zest of it all and trotted along as fast as they could.

We were passing through a valley, when we suddenly heard a shot fired, and I noticed that a bullet whizzed past, just over my helmet. Strangely enough, the feeling of being in danger simply was not there, I never even looked round. Soon afterwards, I asked the evangelist if we could not stop and eat our lunch in that lovely peaceful place. I remember how surprised I was when he answered, almost angrily, that we certainly could not stop *there* to eat, and instead of halting, speeded ahead and hurried us on.

• • • • •

How long after that episode what I am now going to relate occurred I do not remember, it may have been several years. One day, I had a visit from a young Christian man from that district. He had walked for more than seventy miles to see me. Did I remember a trip up to the mountains in the north? We were riding on donkeys and were shot at. Yes, I remembered that journey. Then he told me that he had been standing that day on the mountain slope with a bandit chief, who was known never to miss his aim.

"Shoot!" he had said to the bandit. He took aim and fired. We provided excellent targets riding at donkey-pace, but that time the famous marksman missed.

"Shoot again!" the youth had said.

"No," was the bandit's reply. "I missed, it must be because their time to die has not yet come."

The young man had come the long journey to confess this to me and ask forgiveness for his hatred and intent to murder. We rejoiced together that he had become a believer.

I have often been asked how I account for the bandit's missing his mark that day. I believe that God's angels, mighty in strength, were sent forth to do service for the sake of them that shall inherit salvation.

Angel Sentinels and Two City Walls

I was on a journey and had reached a neighboring station, and was held up there longer than I had expected. It was nearly time for the Chinese New Year and the people were all very busy preparing for the festivities. A communist army was approaching, so the city gates were kept closed. The people were afraid and tensely apprehensive. The Christians in the city met to pray whenever and wherever they could, often in the church.

To everyone's astonishment, however, and without any apparent reason, the army withdrew when it was quite near the city. The only sensible thing for them to do was to attack the city and carry off all the special food that had been cooked for the New Year's feast, it was all but ready to be eaten.

Later the story went that they had seen a large flock of sheep which meant plenty of meat, a prize not to be despised, so they turned aside to round up the flock, but never managed to catch them and finally had to abandon the attempt. By that time they were tired out and a long way from the city.

Another version of the same incident was this: One of the officers in the communist army had asked an acquaintance of one of the church members if there were two walls round the city. He had never seen a city with double walls before, and the strange sentinels on the wall. We who were in the city only knew of one wall and that the soldiery and civil defense guards were not really much to count on compared with the army outside the city.

The prayers of the Christians had gone up to God, who is so often called "The Lord of hosts" in the Bible. It must have been He who took care of us in this time of trouble and delivered us by means of a second wall and the extra guards if that was the right version, or by sending the flock of sheep to draw off the advancing army.

If You Have Faith You Will Come

So ran a sentence in a letter I had received. It challenged me. The letter was about a Women's Bible Course, which had been planned in the autumn and prayed for all through the winter. Now it was spring and the time for it had come. The northern district was swarming with robber bands, the letter said, and the journey, which would take two and a half days, would take me through areas which were especially disturbed just then.

Was it God's will for me to go? If it was, I did not doubt that the Lord of hosts could see me safely through. I had to be sure of His will, so I set aside a day for fasting and prayer. That day led to what to me was an unusual result: my mind and soul were completely dark. Because of this the next day was also given to fasting and prayer, counting on Jesus as the Bread of Life. I felt no hunger that day either, but it closed in even deeper inward darkness. Then I felt assured that the proposed journey was not in God's will for me. As soon as I reached this conclusion, light returned.

A few days later, a special runner came with a message from the northern district to say that the city to which I was to have gone had been captured by the brigands and with it the writer of the letter, one of our women missionaries, and her fellow-workers, a young married couple with an infant child. The little family had been broken up and taken to different places.

Someone immediately took care of the messenger and bathed his feet, which were sore after the forced march, while he related further details of the fall of the city.

The women on the station came quietly in, deeply grieved and rustling the leaves of their Bibles, asking: "What is there in the Bible about this?" It was their first experience of any of their own missionaries being taken by brigands.

We left the others and together we read Psalms 34:7, "The angel of the Lord encampeth round about them that fear him, *and delivereth them.*" And we read some verses in Psalm 91, and prayed earnestly for our friends who were in distress, prayers based on the promises of God, as the women always did after they had learned to know the Word of God. They kept on praying together almost all night. I had not strength for that; it was the hot season and I needed to undress and lie down and continue in prayer on my bed. None of us needed sleep that night. In thought we were with our friends in their trouble, both the missionaries and the Chinese Christians.

The answer to the prayers that ascended to God from our station and many others soon came. In a wonderful way the prisoners were helped through the few days among the bandits. They were released quite suddenly without human intervention; the Hand of the Lord did it. The bandits gave up their claim to the ransom they had demanded.

That time I was not to travel to a bandit-infested area. It had been my heart's desire and my definite prayer that I might not fall into the hands of bandits until I could go through the experience in a God-glorifying way.

Once Again the Lord Was a Wall of Fire

We had had some good days of meetings in the northern part of our field. We had seen the Spirit of God at work, and some troubled souls had entered into the Kingdom of God through the Door—Jesus.

The closing day had come and I was to go home. Early in the morning I felt very unwell with nausea and general discomfort. The missionary in charge of that station said that he did not feel at all happy about my traveling that day, and I felt led to answer: "If I am no better after breakfast, I won't go."

Even before breakfast I felt quite all right and saw no reason for not leaving, although the missionary was obviously anything but pleased about it. He promised to pray for me.

I had not traveled far before I noticed that the road, ordinarily very full of traffic, seemed rather empty that day. The driver was our own man, so he did not object to going on.

One part of the road lay through a rocky pass with high mountains on either side. We were the only travelers when suddenly three armed men jumped out from among some large rocks, behind which they had been hiding. In a few seconds two of them had hold of the bridles of the mules, and the third stood pointing the barrel of his gun at me. I had only time to say in my heart: "Lord, Thou art a wall of fire between him and us." We stared at each other, we two; I do not know for how long, such moments often seem far longer than they are. I was kept perfectly calm and without fear, even peaceful. The wall of fire was there between us. Not a word was spoken. Then the bandit who had been aiming at me turned to the other two and said: "Let go the animals, these people may continue their journey." And as quickly as they had come they disappeared again. I turned to look at the driver, he was pallid with fear. When he regained sufficient courage to speak, his first words were:

"Didn't you realize what sort of men those were?" Seeing me so unafraid he had concluded I did not understand. I was glad of that.

"Yes, immediately, but I could not fear them because we have the wall of fire between us and them, so they could not carry out their evil intent."

He had often heard before, and now he heard again, that *God Himself* protects us like a wall of fire.

The driver was friendly and efficient, but a heathen. Now he was told of the missionary who had been anxious about our journey that morning and had promised to pray for us. We had seen and experienced how his prayers had been answered. This driver had been with us through several deliverances from trouble of various kinds on our journeys. Did he ever believe unto salvation? I do not know, but I hope so, for God in His grace allowed him to experience so often how He Himself guides and delivers.

For Ever, O Lord, Thy Word Is Settled in Heaven

Psalms 119:89

We were four Norwegian missionaries from three different societies who were working together in a series of meetings, when suddenly things grew unsettled. An army had been defeated in battle. As they retreated they were giving vent to their thirst for revenge, and they were now virtually a robber band coming towards the town where we were. Rumor preceded them. They were killing everyone they met. Even women and children out in the fields were being shot down as they passed. That there was some truth in this last statement was confirmed later.

We gathered as many of the Christians as possible for prayer, and late in the evening we four were alone. We repeated the promises, and I found rest in God's concern for us, "He *careth* for you." "Can a woman forget her sucking child, that she should not have compassion on the son of her womb? Yea, they may forget, yet will not I forget thee." "The Lord that hath mercy on thee." "My Father and your Father, and my God and your God." We had found the key, the note of praise, and I suggested to the others that we should go to bed and take what rest we could, even if we had no sleep, before the storm broke.

I had been lying on my bed for some time, repeating the promises of God to myself, "with thanksgiving," when there was a knock at the door. The other three came in and said I must get up and pray. They had never been exposed to this kind of thing before, so their anxiety was natural enough; but they went back to bed to repeat the promises together.

Early in the morning there was shooting quite near us, so we knew that the soldier-bandits had entered the town. We went down to be with the Chinese friends until our turn came to be visited. We were standing together in the open courtyard in front of the missionaries' house just inside the main gate. I realized that as I had had contact with bandits before, I must bear the brunt of this attack when it came.

The butt-end of a gun battered on the gate. I ran and opened it to a solitary soldier, let him in and closed and barred the gate. He was obviously astonished at the unusual scene—a whole group of people calmly standing there, apparently unafraid, although they heard the noise from the streets all round. He was politely invited to come in and have a cup of tea which stood ready in the guestroom just inside the gate.

"You probably don't get much time for food, do you?" he was asked, as he was offered something to eat. He assented, and with a deep sigh said that it was good to sit down in peace and quietness. He thanked us for the tea and murmured:

"I've not stolen this, it is *given* to me."

His questions as to who we were and what we were doing were answered, and he was told about Him, our Lord, who came with salvation and peace. It seemed to be the first time he heard the Name of Jesus.

We were glad no one else knocked at our gate while he was there. Perhaps he himself was most thankful to be left undisturbed to enjoy the unexpected quiet it gave him. When he left he said he would tell the leaders that we were good people and were not to be looted. It sounded improbable that his word could have any effect in the chaotic conditions which prevailed just then, but we actually had no more visitors. Looting soldiers were outlaws, so they never dared stay long in one place. They were all out of the town within twenty-four hours. They left a harried town behind them and in it a little group that believed in the Word of the Lord and had found Him faithful to His promises towards all who put their trust in Him.

It was unutterably marvelous to experience over and over again the peace Jesus spoke of, which the world cannot give. In the midst of confusion and distress one found oneself steadied by such wonderful restfulness of mind, that one did not recognize oneself.

Nothing Happens By Chance to the Lord's People

We were three missionaries on a train, which—to put it mildly—was overcrowded, one a young American and we two Norwegians, from two different societies. The other passsengers were chiefly business people on their way to the capital and so were carrying a good deal of money. As so often happened in those days, the engine broke down and another had to be sent for. There we were, stranded out in the open country with no possibility for all the people to obtain either food or drink. Fortunately it was early day, but it looked as though we were exposed there as an easy prey in case of attack, and robber raids were frequent in those parts.

We three missionaries wondered what ministry the Lord had for us there. We knew that as far as we were concerned it was no mere chance. One of us had to stay on the train to keep our seats and look after our luggage. It was oppressively hot and the young American offered to stay on the train so that we could go outside. The passengers were used to such things, and those of them who had not too much baggage took their little bundles with them and sat down on the rails of the side line to prevent any train that might come from passing without stopping to help us.

We two sat down on the edge of a ditch with our Bibles. It was too hot for us down on the rails, though there was a large congregation there to speak to. But it was best as things were both for us and for a few others. Some seeking souls found us out. On their travels they had heard a little of the Gospel here and there and they were anxious to hear more. The uncertain situation in which we were all placed gave them courage to come to us with questions about their inner problems. They came one at a time, and seemed to take turns so as to be alone with us. It was a good thing for them that we were not surrounded by crowds as we usually were. Several seemed to need just the last bit of help to find the way to Jesus Himself with their burdens. We heard afterwards that one of them had testified in his carriage later that evening to his new-found joy. Was it for the sake of just these that we were detained out on the plains?

At last the longed-for help arrived and we were able to continue our journey. Everyone was sincerely thankful that we did not need to spend the whole night out there.

My Father Runs the Trains

They had been good days with some American missionaries. They had experienced God's great hour and seen the prayers of many years for a work of the Spirit in the church wonderfully answered. I had planned to leave them on a Saturday in order to be in time to keep another appointment. But "higher orders" came to me to wait until the Monday instead. When this was mentioned to the missionary in charge, he immediately answered that it was impossible as there was no train on Mondays. Had I made a mistake? I prayed for clear guidance, and once again the words came: "Leave on Monday." The leader was told that my decision was unchanged, and again answered that it was impossible to leave on a Monday.

This troubled me and for a time I waited quietly upon the Lord in order to understand His way with me, but no other answer to my prayers was given than the same words: "Leave on Monday." I could only respond: "Yes, Lord, and Thou wilt see to my catching a train on Monday." The peace which filled my heart after I had prayed that prayer assured me that all was well.

The missionary who was told of my decision for the third time looked at me with an expression which made no secret of his thoughts.

On the Sunday evening the Chinese pastor there asked for a talk. He had not found peace and asked how he could be saved. I felt it was a great privilege to be allowed to show him the way to Jesus, and realized that it was for this I had been led to postpone my departure.

Very early on Monday morning he came again, this time he was a sinner in need of the Savior, and he received the Savior early that Monday morning.

At breakfast I asked the missionary if he would be kind enough to drive me to the station when I was ready to leave. He gave me to understand that it was a ridiculous request. It was a long way, and the streets of that ancient city were narrow and tortuous, not made for motor traffic. I had heard that he was the only one who could drive a car through those streets, but he obviously did not like having to set out on this crazy business.

When with American speed we drew up at the station, a freight train was standing on the line with steam up. Quick as lightning the missionary dashed into the station and soon returned with a ticket in his hand. With no time for words, my luggage and I were hurried into a brand new railway coach. In the few seconds before the whistle sounded for departure, I heard that the provincial governor had telegraphed for the new carriage he had standing there and it had to be sent immediately at express speed to the capital, the very city I had to reach that Monday in order to catch a north-bound train. We flashed past every station. Never before nor since has it been my lot to travel in such a magnificent carriage, though I once traveled in a royal coach.

I am bound to acknowledge that all through this journey, an incident I had read about Hudson Taylor was a strength to my faith. He had been speaking at a meeting in a city in the United States, and was to take a day's journey the following day to another city where he was to speak in the evening; but he did not have the money for his ticket. Although he was staying with a wealthy man, he did not feel free to mention his need of money, for he had God to confide in.

The coachman had been given orders to be ready in good time in the morning as there was only one train which would get him to his destination in time. That morning, one thing after another went wrong in the stables, and although the coachman was told not to spare the horses, Hudson Taylor was late for the train. His host was very distressed, and could not understand Hudson Taylor's calm. As they stood there, a man came running towards them waving an envelope, delighted that he had managed to catch Hudson Taylor. He in his turn was then able to tell them that this was the money for his ticket.

It was quite incredible to his host that Mr. Taylor should have been staying with him without mentioning that he had not sufficient money for his journey. Mr. Taylor found a train that was going in the direction in which he was to travel and with several changes he would reach his destination, but without the least chance of arriving in time for the meeting. Many wonderful things happened that day and Hudson Taylor arrived in time. He sent a wire to his host: "My Father runs the trains." Those words had laid hold of me that day, when I too was finding them true.

The freight train traveling at express speed made it possible for me to catch the north-bound train, and on that train I met, among others, a missionary with whom I first had pleasant conversation, and who afterwards was a great help to me. I had to make another connection later with a train going west. The second train was crowded and stopped at every station, and it usually reached the junction at which I was to change two hours later than the train I had to catch. The missionary beside me, who had no idea of the desires and prayers in my heart concerning the speed of the train, remarked several times:

"Whatever can be the matter with the engine-driver? People hardly have time to get in and out of the train." Neither of us had seen an ordinary train travel at such speed in China. Finally she began to wonder if the engine driver was drunk, so I told her who it was who was running the train that day and why. At that she stopped worrying.

We arrived exactly in time to allow my fellow-traveler to buy my ticket, while I ran for the train that was just coming in. It was late, "later than it has ever been before" a conductor remarked. There was a fourth train I had to catch that day, going south. I made the connection with ample time for a hot meal before the train left.

And so I arrived in time to keep my appointment. Years before, I had noted that George Müller had boldness to ask that he might arrive in time when faced with impossible travel problems. So I too "drew near with boldness to the throne of grace," as the Bible tells us to do, and in accordance with the promise "received mercy and found grace to help *at the right time*" (Norwegian Version).

With thanksgiving for all these experiences of how the Lord is faithful to keep His own Word, I reached the end of my long journey. A late breakfast eaten in five minutes, and I stood in the pulpit at the appointed hour. Once again we saw in this a testimony to the fact that "His kingdom ruleth over all."

Your Father Knoweth What Things Ye Have Need Of

Matthew 6:8

When I reached the coast to leave for home I was first to meet three new recruits, help them in any way they needed and see them off for the interior. We had to visit the consul and do some shopping both for them and for others on the field.

We were on the go all day long and went everywhere by ricksha. To make sure of their not being lost, it had been impressed upon the three new workers that they must always keep me in sight: it was to be their one concern. They were very careful about it despite the hundred and one fascinating things which drew their attention in the new country; so we managed to get through everything in the three days we had at our disposal.

We had reached the evening of the third day. The new workers were to go on board their boat which was due to leave at midnight. That evening it was I who was not careful enough; but even this was made to work together for good by One who is a Father to His often thoughtless children.

We had five rickshas, one for each of us and one for their suitcases. The new workers still felt themselves responsible in the matter of not losing sight of me, as my ricksha was in front. I remember sitting there profoundly thankful that we had managed to do all we had planned and that everything had gone well, while actually, just then things were going anything but well. It was raining and with their hoods up all rickshas look alike. True, each vehicle had a number at the back; but as we had not used the same ones on our many trips round the city, the men had not noted each other's numbers when we set out that evening.

We did not discover that we had lost each other until only two of us arrived at the ferry which was to take us down to the open water where the steamer was lying. That ferry had to go without us. The next one was the last for that day and would leave in an hour.

There was a moment of complete confusion of mind. Inwardly, questions broke like waves in a storm. Fortunately we quickly reached the only sensible conclusion.

We stood under our umbrellas and prayed to Him who knew where the others were, asking Him to guide them. There was any number of places to which they might be taken. After a while the other two arrived, but not the ricksha with the luggage.

Instead of going with the three to the steamer, I had to give them quick instructions as to how to manage on board a steamer full of Chinese who would not be able to understand them and whose talk would be unintelligible; especially important was the matter of drinking water.

It was eleven o'clock. I stood there wondering what I should do and felt strongly urged to take a ricksha back to the Mission Home. On the way back I kept looking out for the man with the luggage, but never caught sight of him. My heart held only one prayer: "Lord, what wilt Thou do now for Thy children, who need their suitcases for the journey?"

I reached the house at 11.30. At the same moment a policeman arrived, and seeing me about to enter he said he wished to go in too, to ask if anyone there had lost a ricksha full of suitcases. He soon heard the story. He told me that the police had found a man with a ricksha of luggage who did not know where he was supposed to be going.

"Where are the things now?"

They were at a certain police station and it would take about three hours to fetch them from there and get them to the steamer.

"Can I take them out now?"

"No, the office is closed for the night, but it will open tomorrow at 5 a.m."

I was given a paper to say that he had contacted me, and he departed. It was 11.45. Suddenly the thought came: "Phone the steamer."

True, it would be comforting to know that the suitcases were found. I called the number, and heard my own voice asking when the boat was due to leave.

"Unfortunately, we have engine trouble which must be repaired, but we expect to leave tomorrow morning at 8 o'clock."

In my joy I forgot to send the message about the suitcases. I was too happy to sleep and was off by 4 o'clock next morning. My heart was full of thankfulness to our Father in heaven, who has a way of escape for His children in times of trouble, even when the trouble is caused by their own stupidity.

The office was open, and soon the suitcases were standing before me on the counter. The story of the previous evening was repeated.

"The keys?"

"They are with the owners on board the steamer."

"What is in the cases?"

I had not seen their contents, I replied, but I told them what I thought they contained.

Inside the counter there was much discussion as to whether I was to be given the suitcases or not. Outside the counter someone was standing reminding the Lord: "They are Thy children, Lord, and Thou knowest how they need this luggage." They gave me the suitcases in exchange for a receipt on which I was to write my name and address "in my own handwriting."

Full of joy and gladness I proceeded to the steamer with the suitcases. When I arrived they had already taken in the gangway, but the luggage was hauled on board. The three young missionaries had been standing at the rail looking out for their things all the morning, but by this time they had gone below, so they were called up on deck. It was a glorious surprise for them, and at the same time a glorious proof of God's care of His children.

Among Pirates: The Faithfulness of God

Just after my release from twenty-three days' captivity by pirates, it became clear to me that I had not passed through the experience for my own sake only.

This proved true, for without any initiative on my part, the story of those days was published in two editions in China, three in the U.S.A., two in England, several in Sweden, one in Denmark, one in Germany, one in North Africa and one in India.

That it finally appeared in Norwegian as well came about through a prisoner of war, who read a Danish copy of the story on one of the last days of the war in 1945. Before he was shot, he earnestly requested me to publish it in Norwegian "for our young people."

Many who had read it earlier had asked me repeatedly that it might be published "for a new generation." It is my desire that many readers may find the same God, who was my refuge and strength through those days.

"For ever, O Lord, thy word is settled in heaven" (Psalms 119:89).

"Heaven and earth shall pass away, but my words shall not pass away" (Matthew 24:35).

"God is not a man, that he should lie; neither the son of man, that he should repent: hath he said, and shall he not do it? or hath he spoken, and shall he not make it good?" (Numbers 23:19).

"For thou hast magnified thy word above all thy name" (Psalms 138:2).

"God is our refuge and strength, a very present help in trouble" (Psalms 46:1).

· · · · ·

Early in 1929, after a long and very strenuous period of work in the heart of the province of Shansi, I had traveled to Peking. My plan was to spend about ten days really resting. When in need of rest, and I needed it then, I had often been able to shut myself away in the Koks' home—Mr. Kok was the Secretary of the Dutch Legation.

I was expecting to make a long-promised visit to Shantung about April 22nd at the invitation of American friends of the Southern Baptist Mission. Dear friends were there who with one heart and soul had been praying for Revival for a long time. Their prayers were answered later, when revival was given which went deeper than in any of the places where I personally saw revival in China.

The ten days' rest was reduced to only a few days, because as I spent time praying over the journey and the work which lay ahead of me, each day I heard the words:

"If there is a boat on the 19th, go on the 19th."

I wrote to Tientsin to enquire if there was a boat leaving on the 19th, in which case I desired to travel by it. The answer came by wire: "Come."

My packing was quickly done. Summer was near, and, as I was to travel south to warmer parts, all my warm clothes could be left behind in Peking.

In a matter of hours, by midday on the 18th, I was in Tientsin, where I was to stay at the China Inland Mission home. When I arrived they informed me that a boat was going, but all the berths were booked.

My thought was: "If I am to travel by that boat, my Heavenly Father will see to my being given a berth, and if not, He must have some reason for my spending a few days in Tientsin."

In the afternoon a message came to say that the Second Mate was willing to give up his cabin to me for a monetary consideration in addition to the ordinary price of the ticket.

I knew at once that my Heavenly Father had ordered that cabin for me.

No sooner was this matter settled than insistently and repeatedly for several hours I heard the direction: "Go out and buy some apples." I kept thinking, "But I have more than enough luggage as it is, and the journey will only take fifteen hours."

But the apples left me no peace! Perhaps some sick person on the other side of the Gulf of Chihli needs them, was my conclusion;

and, with that thought in mind, I went out and bought all the apples I could find at a Chinese fruit stall, about three pounds altogether.

Next morning, April 19th, while I was praying I was clearly told to deposit in Tientsin all the money I had with me except what I needed to see me to my destination. That was done.

At about 11 o'clock one of the English missionaries went with me to the boat, which we had been informed was to leave at twelve. When he saw the Second Mate's cabin, my escort said: "It is a good thing you will have to spend only one night in there." Altogether I spent twenty-seven.

I had not taken the usual roll of bedding with me on this voyage. The friends on the other side had written to say that if I could manage to sleep one night on hard wooden boards I need not burden myself with bedding. One sleepless night does not matter much, I thought, when I saw it. It is undeniable that it felt hard that first night, but I had plenty of sound sleep on it later, and in the end it even felt fairly comfortable.

"Don't ever call it a *cabin*," remarked an American friend who saw it afterwards, "it looks like an old piano case."

When the ship was well under way, I pulled out a duster and removed a thick layer of dust from the wooden bunk and the little table.

We slipped slowly down the river and at sunset were near the sea, where we lay for some time, coaling.

Almost all the time, I had been on deck talking to the passengers and giving them tracts.

Three of the passengers I had noticed specially. If I had been in my old brigand-infested province of Honan that day, I would have said those three men were brigands. But up here in Tientsin, in the midst of civilization? No, they could not be.

But they were! There were twenty of them altogether who had sailed with us from Tientsin. I had spoken to all those passengers among the rest and had given them tracts.

Late in the evening we put out to sea. There had been stormy weather and the gulf was very rough. We made good speed; and, at dawn the next day, we would see the Shantung coast ahead.

None of us guessed then, that ever since we had put out to sea, two bandits with loaded revolvers had been standing beside the helmsman and that instead of traveling south-east, we were going south-west. They had their own compass with them and had carefully checked the course to see that their orders were obeyed.

Just as land came in sight pistol shots, howls and shrieks were heard and general pandemonium reigned all over the ship. My mind flashed back to the faces of the three men I had noticed the previous day, and at once I knew we had fallen into the hands of pirates.

It was as if a voice said to me just then: "This is the trial of your faith," and at those words I was conscious of an inner, warm, living, glad willingness to walk also this part of the road with the Lord. "O that He may succeed in keeping me close to Himself," was my one conscious desire in the midst of all the noise and confusion.

More pirates had come on board by that time, about sixty of them we heard afterwards. These were the permanent force; we often had visits from smaller bands later and at such times there was a good deal of disturbance on board.

The first word that came to me was Isaiah 41:10, a word I had often needed when in the province of Honan. I repeated it aloud in the way I had so often done earlier: "Fear thou not, Marie: for I am with thee: be not dismayed, Marie; for I am thy God: I will strengthen thee; yea, I will help thee, Marie; yea, I will uphold thee with the right hand of my righteousness."

Long before, when I was in Honan Province, the Lord had told me not to be afraid, and I had answered Him: "I will obey, Lord, I will not be afraid."

Soon all cabin doors were forced open and the passengers ordered out on deck. I heard them go out. They were told to leave all their possessions in their cabins. The sea was rough and the waves very high.

My door was wrenched open too. "The Blood of the Lamb is sprinkled on my doorposts" came to mind as they pulled at my door. This line of an old well-known Danish hymn sounded continually in my heart, especially at first when the pirates were wildest.

Over and over again they ordered me out of my cabin, but I stayed where I was. I knew I had been given that cabin in answer to prayer and I felt I should stay in it. If I had gone out, I should have landed in the hold of the ship with all the other passengers. There were several hundred of them.

Because I had not taken a roll of bedding with me, I was fully dressed, which was fortunate. I was the only Christian and the only foreigner on board.

Between each order to come out of my cabin (the pirates never took time to see their order was obeyed) the wonderful promises of God came to me, gently and refreshingly, like spring showers. I received them and thanked God. From that moment *I* was no longer *I*, but another person altogether, who was often a source of amazement to me. "Then the strength which has been promised for each day's needs means all this," I often whispered to myself with a deeply thankful heart.

At length one of the pirates, a man of about thirty, took time to stop in my cabin. He asked if I had a watch. I had entirely forgotten about my things, I had been so absorbed in considering the promises of God. I stretched out my wrist and let him look at it. I was sitting on the wooden bunk. He whispered confidentially: "Hide it or you will lose it." I took it off and put it under a bundle of clothes which I had been using as a pillow. He saw me do this, then he went away.

A little later, another came in, quite a young lad, perhaps seventeen or eighteen.

"Have you a watch?"

"Yes, I have."

"Have you given it to anyone?"

"No, I haven't."

"Will you give it to me?"

"No, I can't do that. We never give such valuable presents to people we don't know."

"Yes, but don't you understand that if you give it to me, I will be your friend?"

"Thank you, but I don't want friends like you. I've never had that kind of friend."

"But don't you understand that if I am your friend, I will ask the others to protect you?"

He jumped up, held his pistol to my forehead and shouted angrily:

"I'll shoot you."

"No, you can't shoot me whenever you like. My God has said: 'No weapon that is formed against thee shall prosper. . . this is the heritage of the servants of the Lord.'" And I explained clearly to him what it meant that before he could shoot me, the living God must give him permission.

Again he jumped up and held his pistol to my forehead:

"I can; I'll shoot you."

"No, you can't." The promise was repeated to him four or five times. I had the great joy of hearing him say that promise almost every day for the next twenty-three days. It usually came in a scornful tone:

"Just think, she says I can't shoot her whenever I like because her God has said that no weapon that is formed against her shall prosper."

All natural human fear either of him or his pistol was simply taken away from me.

And now the man who had told me to hide my watch came back. He threw out the younger pirate and asked to be allowed to look at the watch. It was handed to him.

"Foreigners have good watches, this is a good one," he said.

"Yes, it is."

"I'll give you twenty dollars for it."

"No, I wouldn't sell it even if you offered me two hundred dollars for it, because your money is not honestly come by. I've never used money of that kind. I wouldn't touch a single dollar of your money."

"Then I'll give you another watch in exchange for this one; it is not quite as good, but I'll give you another."

"No, thank you, if you give me another in exchange, it will be a watch you have stolen from someone else, so I couldn't use it."

"Well then, there is no help for it," and he sighed and went away with my watch. In the doorway he turned round and said:

"You gave me this watch of yours, didn't you?"

"No, I didn't. If you take it, you have robbed me."

He took it away.

A little sigh went up: "O Lord, I can do without it, and I know I can have another instead, but it would be nice to know what the time is while I am on board this ship."

About half an hour later another pirate came in. He looked tired. He turned my largest suitcase up on its end, sat down heavily on it and said I need not be afraid.

"Do you think I look afraid? "

"No, you don't."

He told me that some of the pirates had belonged to General Chang's army in Shantung, but they felt they were not receiving sufficient pay in the army, so they were now earning their living in this way and making more money. "You needn't be afraid; we shall protect the ship, that is why we are on board."

"Oh yes, I see that," I laughed. "But seriously, do you call this earning a living? I don't. I call it robbery, and you are doing violence to your own conscience."

We talked in sober earnest till it became uncomfortably personal for him and he rose hastily, asking:

"Have they taken anything from you?"

"Yes, my watch."

"Who took it?"

Fortunately I could tell him. He said he would bring it back, but although I did not believe he meant it, to my surprise and delight, he did.

When he handed me my watch he leaned forward and said: "I'll give you a piece of advice. Don't leave this cabin. If you do, you'll never get it back, and they will take away what you have here. If they come and want to take anything from you, just tell them that the General said they were not to rob you."

This pirate was always friendly after that, though he never entered the cabin again. I had a feeling that he must have been educated at one of the mission schools of Shantung.

They soon began coming one after another, and the first thing they always asked for was my watch.

"It was taken from me once, but has been given back, so you can't have it. Besides, the General says you are not to rob me."

It was easy to see the effect those words produced, but a few tried to catch me by saying:

"Who is the General?"

"You know yourself, so I needn't tell you," was my usual reply.

"I've not heard him forbid it," one or two remarked.

The returning of my watch led to my taking a promise long known and loved and making it my prayer of faith in a definite way, the promise in Malachi 3:18: "Then shall ye *return, and discern* between the righteous and the wicked, between him that serveth God and him that serveth him not." (In Norwegian: "Then shall ye again *see the difference between...* him that serveth God and him that serveth him not.")

· · · · ·

An intense desire filled me that the hundreds of passengers and the thirty-five members of the crew, all of them heathen, might see that I had a living, almighty God. It was wonderfully fulfilled to the glory of His name.

· · · · ·

In the evening of the first day a junk came and lay alongside the ship. It was loaded with guns and ammunition. After these supplies had been taken on board, we lay still or moved up and down the coast. They captured and plundered every boat they saw. We were Vikings! I could see it all from my door which had to be kept ajar so that I might get fresh air. The little cabin window could not open. Large cargoes of corn, salt, flour and a great deal besides were captured. Most of it was carried ashore.

I can still see the many boatmen standing scared and helpless, intimidated by pistol shots which were fired into the air while they were robbed. In the five days I watched this going on, our legendary Vikings were stripped of the last shreds of their glory in my mind; for *this was how* they did it!

The ammunition was stored in the cabin next to mine. On the other side in the purser's cabin, they had their headquarters, where their councils of war were held. Through the thin boards of the wall I could hear everything they said.

"Shut the foreigner's cabin door."

I heard someone give the order. Obviously they did not wish me to see how much ammunition they were taking on board. I had begun counting the boxes.

"Shut the door and lock it," I heard again from outside. The door was slammed to and someone fumbled with the lock, someone who did not understand locks. The key snapped before it locked the door. "Thank God!" was my involuntary response from inside the cabin.

A couple of hours later—the door was ajar again—two of the pirates came and stood leaning on the railing outside my door. They kept looking in, speaking in eager whispers to each other. I had seen a good many bandits in the interior of China, but never any more hideously repulsive than those two. The subject of their whispered conversation was not hard to guess. One of them pushed the other into my cabin, closed the door and tried to lock it, but the key had been broken.

I felt as if the devil himself had come in. His face, neck and hands were covered with horrible, open, stinking sores. He sat down on my suitcase so close to me that I felt his warm breath on my face.

I sat repeating to myself the promise that had become so precious to me in the bandit-ridden province of Honan: "The angel of the Lord encampeth round about them that fear him, *and delivereth them.*"

Another promise came back to me again at that moment: "For I, saith the Lord, will be unto Jerusalem a wall of fire round about." Yes, and He would be a wall of fire round about me. He was a wall of fire between me and the horrible pirate sitting there.

Many years earlier the Lord had allowed me to see that wall of fire. I was awakened in the middle of the night by two sharp blows on my shoulder, and the words sounded aloud and distinctly: "The Lord is a wall of fire round about His people." Then it was as though the roof was lifted off the house and I saw that I was surrounded by fire, a high, impenetrable wall of fire. From beyond the wall thousands of arrows came flying towards me. They came so thickly that they darkened the sky, but tongues of flame shot up and consumed everyone of them. None reached me. I wept. "Lord, I never knew it was in this way Thou art round about Thy people."

In this difficult hour, that experience was vividly brought back to mind and I thought: "The Lord is round about me like that to-day: I am untouchable, invulnerable."

To my own amazement it was I who began the conversation. It came perfectly naturally, without reflection:

"Is your mother still living?"

"Yes."

"How old is she?"

"Fifty-one."

"No, really! Then she and I are just the same age."

He was then asked about his father, his brothers and sisters and other relatives. We had a long talk. At my request he opened the door again—without fresh air the stench was unendurable. Having done so, he sat down again.

I soon found that he had heard the Gospel. He knew a missionary too of whom he said:

"He is truly a good man; there isn't a better in the world." I found out later that that missionary was one of the rare souls, a truly godly man.

He also knew some Christians in his home town. I think we talked to each other for a whole hour. He was told the truth about his life; and he heard too about the Savior who cared for so many lost robbers and made all things new for them. He had heard quite a lot before and he sighed, even groaned a couple of times, and his eyes were blinded by tears when he finally slipped quietly out of the cabin. I did not see him again.

Those days and nights we had been Vikings and the noise had been indescribable. The pirates terrorized their victims by noise. Sleep was out of the question. After five such days and nights, my head felt as if it would burst.

"Lord, I ask for sleep, I must have some sleep now. Thou hast created me with a need of sleep. For years Thou hast kept me in health through making my sleep sweet!" (Proverbs 3:24). My silent requests were made in words like these.

Praise God, before long—it seemed within a few minutes—deathly silence fell. It was as though the pirates were no longer on the ship. I was too sleepy to look out and see what had happened: "The Lord God has let sleep fall upon them so that I may have some peace," was my last thought, and then I myself was asleep.

From that time there was a marked difference in the situation. After that we heard only an occasional pistol shot, and there was less of the wild looting and of the ceaseless running to and fro. The ship was placed in a secluded bay with flat stretches of sand and plains on three sides and the ridges of high hills on the fourth. Later I discovered that the sea lay behind those ridges. We were in one of the arms of the Yellow River delta, Taoerho.

· · · · ·

For the first five days and nights it was like swimming upstream against a strong current, although strength sufficient was given for this. Later it was like floating along, carried by the current down a river, with a full assurance that I would be swept in to the bank in time.

There was a reason for this change. At first, those I had left behind in Tientsin took it for granted that I had safely reached port. The friends who were expecting me had traveled down to the coast to meet me. They could not understand the delay, and after waiting for a day and a half they had been obliged to go home again. All they knew was that the ship had left Tientsin according to schedule but had not arrived.

By the fifth day both these groups of friends had been told that the ship had been seen with a crew of pirates on board, out of its regular course. Telegrams were sent in all directions and a stream of prayer began to ascend, both from missionary colleagues and from the Chinese Christians. The effect was wonderful.

I saw nothing of the ship's regular crew except the "tea-boy." A couple of times a day he brought me a jug containing a pint and a half of "white tea"—boiling water! On the second day I found my cabin had fittings for an inner door of wire netting. The tea-boy knew where this door was and promised to bring it at dusk, while the pirates were smoking their opium. He was as good as his word, and at my request he brought some screws and a screwdriver so that we could fix it up. A hook was fixed on the inside, which meant I could shut or open at will and keep it "locked" and still have the air.

Once more I thanked God that He had chosen this cabin for me, where I could be alone. All the other cabins except the Captain's contained several berths, and the pirates had seized them all.

Before the wire netting door was put in, the pirates had free access to my little world; but after it came, if the door did not open at a push they would pass on. Whenever they asked to be allowed to come in, I opened to them. Then I felt I had my opportunity to appeal to their consciences and preach the Gospel to them. There was still no feeling of fear and it never assailed me.

Somehow, most of my visitors did not seem to feel comfortable in my cabin, and after the first ten days or so they stopped coming; but at mealtimes they would bring their food bowls and sit down on the deck outside my door to eat. That was my opportunity to speak to them. Those who could read were given tracts. Often one of them would read aloud and another try to explain what was read, and then I always had the final word. Questions were often put both on my side and theirs, and through all this I felt assured that I had been sent among them in order that they might hear the gospel.

They were always offering me food—lobster, crayfish, tinned goods of every kind, fish, chicken—all stolen goods. Gratefully I noticed that I had no appetite for any of it.

The deck outside my cabin was very narrow, but they would practice cycling there for hours on end. They had found two or three new cycles in the hold of the ship.

The first few days they all wore glasses which they had stolen from the passengers, but the fashion did not last long and a few days later they all appeared unspectacled again.

The pirates all turned out wearing one silk garment on top of another—the passengers' clothes, of course. The twelve women among their prisoners had more than enough to do, altering this stolen wear to fit them.

"You are all so beautifully dressed," I said one day to one of them.

"Yes, here on board. We never have our fine clothes for long. When the military are at our heels, we throw away one garment after another, usually we have nothing left but a pair of trousers. Lightly come and lightly go," and he laughed. It was literally to be so this time too.

It looked as though they practiced steering the ship each day. It was just a toy in their hands and it was a real miracle that we did not get into trouble through this game of theirs.

As to food, the passengers were well content with the hot meals the pirates served them twice a day. The food had all been looted from the junks. They were given only the simplest Chinese fare. For me it was different. I felt I could not eat stolen food. The mere thought made me feel sick, so there was never any question about it in my mind. Not until later did I realize that God guided me in this, for in the end, the fact that I had not tasted the food they offered me was my salvation—from the human point of view.

Long before this happened, God had provided all that was necessary. I had the apples, and glad I was now that I had them. The pirates often asked me if I had any pears or any oranges, because in that case they wanted them. Not once was I asked if I had any apples.

For a long time I had four boxes of chocolates and sweets in my luggage. Ever since February they had been arriving, sent from four different countries. Each time I wanted to share them with others there was the inner voice: "Keep them for an emergency." It was just impossible to part with them, and I even took myself to task: "You are getting old and stingy, Marie, to think you are traveling about with all this in your luggage!" The day before I left Peking, while I was packing, the Koks' youngest daughter was in my room and I gave her one of the boxes of chocolates. Just then her mother came in and quickly took it away from the child: "Take it back and hide it quickly, she can't eat chocolates," she said.

I had a packet of biscuits too, about fifteen altogether. This had also been given me some time before, and it was the same story with them. "Keep them for an emergency."

How I thanked God now that I had it all. I divided it up in rations and it lasted for nine days. After it became clear to me that it was not the Lord's will for me to eat the pirates' food, I knew He would have some way out when I needed more. The God of Elijah still has ravens at His command. He took worry away, but it was exciting. It was going to be interesting to see how He would supply my need.

On the tenth day, early in the morning before it was light, there was a gentle scratch at my door which was closed just then. I jumped down from my wooden bunk. My heart sang: "This is the raven!" (1 Kings 17:4).

It was the Second Mate. Up till then I had not seen him, nor any of the ship's crew except the tea-boy. He asked me in a whisper:

"Have you any food?"

"No, I haven't."

"Let me come in then, the guard is on the other side of the ship. I have a box full of eggs in here and a tin of cakes, you can have it all. I bought it in Tientsin with my own, honestly earned money."

Wonderfully the words were fulfilled, "Before they call, I will answer." In the prepared cabin, food was prepared too.

The Second Mate pulled out the boxes, which were hidden among buckets of paint, old shoes, empty paraffin tins and all sort of old lumber.

From that day he came every morning unasked, when the guard was on the other side of the ship, took two or three eggs and, putting them in his pocket, went away. A little later he came back with the boiled eggs. My ration was one egg for breakfast, one or two eggs for dinner and one egg for supper; and besides this, one sweet cake in the forenoon and one in the afternoon. This supply of food lasted exactly as long as our captivity.

I asked the Lord to transform this simple fare into all the body requires, and I had no trouble at all on account of the monotonous diet. When I had eaten my small ration, I felt so satisfied that I would not have eaten any more if I had had it.

The first days after my release I did not seem to need food. Not very much of the first bowl of rice that was given me was eaten; but a few shrimps offered me the first day we were free tasted wonderful. I did not know how long I sat sucking them. Then I realized for the first time that I had not tasted salt for twenty-three days.

The pirates kept coming to ask if I would not have some of their food. They said I could order whatever I liked and they would try to get it for me. They often came and offered me tinned fruit.

"No, thank you; it is all stolen goods and whatever I asked for, you would only go and steal from other people and I can't eat stolen food," was my usual answer.

They said I would die of starvation, but I told them my Father in heaven was able to keep me alive.

One day one of the pirates came to see me. He was very ill with dysentery. With tears in his eyes he began:

"Pastor" (they always called me that, possibly because it was the only title they knew for a foreigner), "when I eat, I can hardly swallow my food for thinking of you eating nothing all this time. If I could get something for you, I would, but there is nothing to get here. If I could go ashore, I would buy food for you with your own clean money."

This man, I felt, must be comforted.

"My Heavenly Father looks after me, He gives me food every day," I told him.

"What does He give you?"

"He has given me apples, chocolate, biscuits, eggs and cakes." Those five words were spoken in Norwegian.

"I don't understand," he said, "but you look well."

Just as I was leaving Peking on the morning of April 18th, a parcel from Norway reached me. It was a belated Christmas parcel and had been posted in plenty of time to reach me before Christmas. Where it had been all the time, I do not know. But I do know that if it had come a single day earlier it would have been put away in the attic of the Austrian legation, where the rest of my woolen clothes were being preserved in mothballs for the summer.

At first I groaned over the addition to my luggage, but how thankful I was afterwards for the contents of that parcel—a cardigan and a pair of woolen stockings. They were a great comfort. It was bitterly cold on the stormy days out in the Gulf of Chihli and later, in the windy estuary of the Yellow River. That parcel was prepared beforehand and the day of its arrival, too.

While I was packing for the journey, the post brought me five fat bundles of newspapers from Norway. They had been posted by five different people, each of whom thought I ought to know all about the wedding of our Crown Prince. Inwardly protesting and greatly wishing to leave them behind, I found room for those five packets in my luggage, increasing its bulk most unreasonably. But I was thankful later; I simply could not have managed without them. Thick layers of newspaper, fastened inside my raincoat with safety-pins, provided a warm coverlet, and with my traveling rug kept me warm at night.

One of the pirates stood on guard outside my door at night to prevent me from escaping. He usually sat on the doorstep of the ammunition room, and probably had to guard both that and me. Two or three times every night he allowed the beam of a powerful torch to play over me. I slept well and peacefully between these searchlight inspections.

Those twenty-three days I gained considerable insight into how the younger lads were taught the trade. I was next door to headquarters, and they repeatedly forgot I could hear everything that went on in there. I learned that the shooting we were always hearing was meant to intimidate the victims and prepare the way for the extortion of money. I myself, however, was never exposed to this, though they gave me to understand that they intended to get a great deal of money for me when the time came. The other passengers were continually threatened till they consented to write for ransom money.

One of the pirates, a man of about sixty, was stone blind. But he, too, robbed people. He went about feeling the passengers all over and then commanded them to hand over whatever he wanted.

"Isn't he rather in your way?" I asked one day.

"No, he is the most useful man we have, we can't do without him."

"How is that?"

"Well, you see, when we are pursued on land he sits down with his beggar's bowl and bag, and our pursuers always stop and ask him if he has 'seen' us, and he always directs them the wrong way. We find him again all right; it is never difficult for him to discover which way we have gone."

What I missed most on board was water to wash in. Occasionally I was offered water in which four or five pirates had washed first, but I always declined with thanks. A few drops of my "white tea" on a handkerchief was not quite adequate on hot days, though even this was easier than one would have expected.

On about the tenth day, two Red Cross men came on board. They were given a somewhat warm welcome, many warning shots were fired. Possibly they had been sent by the ship's company to see how we were faring as to food supplies. I was allowed to send a postcard which I had by them, but they probably never got ashore. The next day I was asked if it was to my King I had written.

"No, I wouldn't send a postcard to my King; I would write a letter and put it in a fine large envelope." They thought that reasonable enough.

At about that time I was allowed more freedom. I had made "the little General," their chief, understand that I needed more fresh air and exercise. "But you must give your men orders to keep to the other side of the ship while I am out walking, otherwise they will go into my cabin, and you know that won't do." He gave the order immediately that it was to be as I wished. After that there was no difficulty about this, and it made a difference to my comfort while on board.

As I have said, they never demanded ransom money from me, nor did they mention in my hearing where they meant to get it from, but they often said:

"Don't you know you are worth a lot of money?"

"Yes, I know that. You have probably had to do with foreigners before, but they may not all have been worth as much as I am. I am a child of God, and the Kingdom of God belongs to me. Truly, I am worth much money."

"Yes, and we want a lot for you."

"You won't get it. Not a single dollar will you get for me. I am God's child and my God has promised to set me free without price." Isaiah 45:13 was always quoted to them when this subject was brought up.

They made deliberate efforts to make me impatient, usually by telling me they meant to hold me captive for a long time. Perhaps they hoped I would offer them ransom money.

"Don't you ever get impatient?" they would ask me.

"Do I look impatient?"

"No, that's just what you don't look. Whatever we do, we can't provoke you. Aren't you longing to go ashore and get away from us?"

"No, I'm not, and I thank God for that. He sent me to China to preach the Gospel, and now He wants me here with you to preach the Gospel to you, so I'll stay as long as it is His will. It is He who has arranged this."

"Can you understand such peace?" I heard them say to each other. "We can see it in her face. How different the other passengers look. They get more and more impatient every day." I knew it was true and thanked God that they had discerned the difference.

It was on about the ninth day that two men came on board. I was never told who they were, but from their conversation I guessed they came from the ship's company.

They were taken to headquarters, and I heard the pirates demand $200,000 for the ship. The two men asked:

"Can't the foreigner pay half?"

At this the chief grew irritable: "Now, let us arrange this quickly, for truth to tell the foreigner is near death. She has not been able to eat anything all this time."

Profound silence.

As I did not want the men to go back with the report that I was lying at death's door, I went out on deck. The door to headquarters was standing open. The chief was sitting with his back to the door and did not see me. The other two saw me. I nodded and smiled, so they saw I was alive all right. I do not think the others sitting further in saw me.

In the days that had passed the Lord had wonderfully fulfilled the promise in Malachi 3:18. I was the only passenger who was allowed to keep any money. I was repeatedly asked how much money I had, just as the other passengers were. I told them exactly how much I had with me, and each time I added: "You can't take it away from me, I am going to use it for my ticket when I continue my journey." But it was not due to any words of mine that I was allowed to keep my money, I fully realize that. There was to be a difference, that was why.

"Now we have looted everything from all the others, let us rob the foreigner too," I heard more than once from headquarters.

"Is there anything to take? Which of you wants to wear a woman's clothes? She only has books and papers. What would you do with them?" was often the answer. The Chinese women's clothes had been taken from them, but there was to be a difference between one who served God and those who served Him not.

A soft, warm woolen shawl I had was one thing several of the pirates coveted. They would pick it up and cuddle it to their faces. Sometimes they turned round quietly without a word and went off with it, but none of them got further than the door. They would come back with it, equally quietly, lay it down with a sigh and go away.

At least half the pirates fell in love with my coat. They would hold it up against themselves to see if it fitted them. Some, who thought it a good fit, would begin to slip out silently with it but they never went beyond the door. There was to be a difference.

I had two strong little leather suitcases and one larger cheap one. Every single suitcase both large and small belonging to the other passengers had been cut up to make holsters for their pistols—they were the latest fashion among the pirates. All my three suitcases stood there in full view. Over and over again I was asked if the larger one was real leather, "because if it is, we want it for our pistols," but never once did they ask about the smaller cases. It was as if they did not see them, yet they were quite large enough for holsters. There was to be a difference, that was all.

After only a few days on board the whole ship was a pestilential stinking hole, and the drinking water was almost undrinkable. I was probably the only person on board who knew how serious the situation was. Something had to be done and I must see that it was done, that soon became clear to me. But would they listen to me? "Who maketh winds His messengers," came to me. Yes, I thought, and He can make the pirates my servants. It came as a completely new thought and gave assurance in prayer.

The opportunity prayed for soon came. I needed to speak to one of the big men. When I was standing outside my cabin door taking a breath of air, the chief and his second-in-command came by on their way to the opium den. They stopped, the chief evidently out of humor. He was always a man of few words and his companion a courteous man of the world. When I asked where the Captain was, they answered:

"In his cabin."

"You have locked him in?"

"Yes, we have."

"Then I understand why the crew is not doing their work; but since you and I and all the other passengers are to live on this ship, you must see that the decks are rinsed and scoured every day; that is always done on ships of this kind."

Their eyes wandered over the deck and then came back to me.

"What you wish shall be done."

A pirate came running up and was told what "the Pastor" had said and forthwith sent with orders to the crew. After that they performed their task, and it made life a great deal pleasanter—to me at any rate.

They saw to the drinking water too. The man who had had charge of that detail was found and reinstated in his office. At my request the passengers were allowed to come up on deck in turns for air and exercise. The large side doors to the pestilential hold were thrown open, and the prisoners were permitted to see to the ventilation of their quarters themselves. Later, when the heat grew intense, awnings were put up as soon as the pirates were brought to see it was necessary.

"It is you who have been in command on this ship, I hear," said the Captain when we met again after our release, and the imprisoned passengers knelt on the deck to express their gratitude. "Thank you, thank you, we know that things were very different for us because you were here on board." They knew about the difference.

The last five days the pirates kept up a ceaseless discussion as to how they were to take me away from the ship; they knew they would soon have to leave. There were large "geese" (I guessed they meant gunboats) outside the estuary. The last three days among them were exciting. Once on each of those days their plans for removing me from the ship were completely ready to be put into execution.

About fifty junks lay moored near the steamer. The pirates' bedding and sacks of flour and rice had already been transferred to these junks. I saw baskets of eggs, leeks and poultry being carried down and placed in them.

The chief's junk was to move in front with a smaller junk on either side followed by my junk with guards on board and two smaller junks on either side.

It was a warm day of brilliant sunshine. We were to leave the ship at three o'clock in the afternoon. They spent hours that day discussing how they would carry me off and where they would take me. The places they mentioned were all unknown to me. Their arguments were carried on in loud tones. I was reminded of the words: "The heathen rage." Yes, how true that is, I thought. Then I remembered another verse of the same Psalm: "He that sitteth in the heavens shall laugh." Suddenly I felt free to laugh with Him. It was not in presumption, it was holy laughter. I had to check myself from laughing aloud, lest the pirates should hear me, and think I had lost my reason.

But I had reason for laughter. Two wonderful promises had become a living reality to me that day: "In the covert of thy presence shalt thou hide them from the plottings of man" (Psalms 31:20 RV) and "Shall the prey be taken from the mighty, or the lawful captive delivered? But thus saith the Lord, Even the captives of the mighty shall be taken away, and the prey of the terrible shall be delivered: for I will contend with him that contendeth with thee" (Isaiah 49:24-25).

I could not remember having read that second promise, and did not know where it was in the Bible, but I had asked God for a promise to "speak to my condition." It was wonderful. From that hour, I dared to tell the pirates that they would never manage to carry me off with them, and I told them what my God had said.

Just before the hour at which they had decided to go, a storm arose, a mighty whirlwind, which seemed to rage only round the ship. The junks were dashed against the hull till they were almost crushed. Without waiting for orders, the men in the junks loosed their mooring-ropes and made for shelter ashore.

After that storm, I did not hear a sound for several hours, nor see a single person. I believe the pirates were firmly convinced that it was my God who was calling them to account. When the storm had passed, the hour for opium-smoking was too near to allow of anything more being done that day.

On the following day the same hour was fixed for our departure from the ship as they had planned the day before; but just then some spies who had been sent out returned. There was a long, loud discussion on the foredeck, out of my hearing. All I could understand was that there was something they could not agree about. Then opium time came again and no more was done that day.

The day before our release, they were ready to leave for the third time, again at the same hour. This time I heard the order given to one of the men: "Go and tell the foreigner that she must get into the junk now, so that we can get away."

I jumped down from my bunk. I shall never forget the sound of his steps approaching my cabin door. "Lord, what wilt Thou do now?"

The door was roughly opened. We stood staring at each other, he at me and I at him. I think we stood like that for five minutes. Perhaps it was not so long, but they were the longest minutes of my life.

He did not cross the threshold. Without a word, he slammed the door to and went away. I heard him say: "You may do what you like to me, but I can't tell her that she is to be wronged a second time." I stood praying that he might not lose his life for those words. Some important reports from their spies came in, much discussion followed, and probably both he and I were forgotten for the rest of that day.

It was a strange evening. Unexpectedly and unplanned, I had a meeting with the pirates which lasted for two or three hours. It was the most remarkable meeting in my experience. Words and strength were given me. The Spirit of God was there. There was the silence which falls when the Word is being given room in hearts. They were brought to see themselves that day.

"We are bad, only bad. We were born bad. We do evil from morning to night and from night till morning. You were born good; you don't hate us, everyone else hates us."

They all agreed that it was so. What joy to be able to tell them that I was born with the same evil heart as they, and then tell them of Him who came to save us all and give us a new heart. They would not easily forget that evening.

On the twenty-third day, a Sunday, at three o'clock in the afternoon, we heard the sound of guns. "That means we are found," I said aloud on my wooden bunk. Ever since the early hours of the morning, the pirates had been busy hauling heavy, rusty iron plates up on deck and fixing them along the railings. Clearly the ship was being prepared for defense.

After we heard the guns, there was a great deal of running about and soon most of the pirates left the ship. The captain was ordered out of his cabin, I was told later, and a race up-river began, our ship ahead and the gunboat following.

Before long the pirates saw that the gunboat was gaining on us. From the moment the guns first sounded, I had heard them say over and over again outside my door:

"We must take the foreigner with us. . . . As things stand now, we can't go away without the foreign face with us. . . . They won't dare to shoot when they see we have the foreigner with us."

The last voice I heard said: "Under these circumstances it is no use taking the foreigner. She has eaten nothing for twenty-three days, she can't walk, much less run as we must now." Was that voice not that of the man who had brought me back my watch?

Then the pirates left the ship.

Quick as thought, I was on deck. The Captain turned the ship and we steamed downstream towards the gunboat. Some of the pirates were already a long way across the sandbank. They were running for their lives, and their pathway was strewn with the garments they threw away as they ran.

The last of them, who were still in the junks, were all facing landwards, not once did they look back at the ship. And then they too ran for all they were worth, though they were not followed by anything but a few warning shots.

I sighed to think that my work among them was finished. I had become perfectly willing to be carried off by them, if only I might see some of them saved; but I did not believe that I would be carried off, as I had my Bible and its promises to rely upon.

There was not time to stand long in thought. The passengers! I must go down and see them. They were all sitting like images in stone with bowed heads looking down, only looking down. I stood on the ladder leading down to the hold: "Come up, come up, all the pirates have gone." No one moved, no one even looked up. I repeated my words. Still they sat silent and immovable. "I am the foreigner, come up, come up." That roused them, and soon they were all over the deck, gazing with their own eyes at the pirates running across the sandy flats. Then I saw a sight which I only saw that once in China. They began to laugh and cry for joy and to embrace one another. They were quite wild with delight, and had to find some expression for all their pent-up emotions. They evidently thought their behavior strange themselves.

"We have been sitting with a sword in our hearts for twenty-three days," they said apologetically.

· · · · ·

The pirates took twenty of the passengers with them, most of the women among them; but they came back the same evening before it was quite dark. The twelve women had come to my cabin every day, at the hour when the pirates smoked their opium and slept off its effects. The arrangement had been made through the tea-boy. It was

94

the best hour in the day to me. None of them had heard the Gospel before, and they were in trouble, so their hearts were open.

When these women came back that evening, they came running to me saying eagerly: "We prayed that the foreigner's God would deliver us, and He has delivered us." They were radiant. We had a lovely time of praise in my cabin after that. Later some of the men told me that one of the pirates had arranged for the women to be put in a room by themselves, and had told his companions that they were under his protection: "Only across my dead body do you enter here," he had said.

By the description given, it must have been the man who brought back my watch. When he astonished me so by bringing it, I had followed an impulse of the moment and told him he must be responsible for the few women on the ship and see that they came to no harm.

When we were alongside the gunboat, a couple of the officers came across to our ship, congratulating themselves over having found us at last. We were told that it would take about four days to complete their enquiries into the whole affair. After that we could disembark at the port of our original destination.

· · · · ·

Next morning I went across to the gunboat to send a telegram to our Norwegian authorities in China. They made all sorts of difficulties about this, though they were very kind to me otherwise.

"I wouldn't care to be in your shoes when our consul hears that I asked you to send this wire and you refused to do so." The wire was sent.

They served tea and cakes and pressed me urgently to move over to the gunboat. They showed me the best cabin, which, they said, was prepared and ready for me. It was obviously a disappointment to them that I did not accept. It would have been a proud moment when they entered harbor with a live proof of well-executed service on board.

The gunboat was thoroughly modern all through, at any rate in the eyes of one who was not a naval expert. It was wonderfully clean. The officers I saw all seemed to be confirmed opium smokers though they were young. The ratings looked healthy and strong (in the Royal Navy, "ratings" refer to those who hold a military rank).

They said they had been looking for us for weeks. Every bay in the Gulf of Chihli had been searched several times and finally they had reached the conclusion that we could only be hiding in the delta of the Yellow River, though ships did not usually go there. They had captured the crews of five junks, shut them up in separate cells and examined them and in this way they had found out our position. These men had been forced to point out the best pilot among them who could take the gunboat into the Taoerho. They would all be set free when this man had performed his task, not before.

I simply *had* to go back and have the next few days with my fellow-passengers. They were wonderful days. Their hearts were so open. They literally fought for the tracts and Bible portions I had. "It feels as if we had our mother on the ship with us," I heard more than once those days, but the best thing I heard was this: "Your God has helped you through this, we have seen that, but none of our gods have helped us." Thank God, they were in no doubt at all as to the difference.

At last, after twenty-seven days, we landed at our destination. But there was fighting going on in that part of the province and we could hear the roar of cannon across the water. The harbor-master came on board. He was a Christian. He told me it was impossible to land there and promised to enquire what could be done. A few hours later he came back.

"You have been long enough on this ship, but in a couple of hours a boat will be leaving for Dairen in Manchuria. We have taken a first class cabin for you on it. Here is your ticket. It is paid for, and I am glad it is my privilege to show you that there are people in this province who are different from those you have met with. May God bless and keep you."

The unexpected guest who arrived at the Danish missionaries' home in Dairen was made very welcome. We had only exchanged a few words, when Emil Jensen and his wife said: "Now we really must praise the Lord for His mercy," and we did, from full hearts. It was lovely to have a bath, a meal, a bed and loving care, but best of all was the communion of the saints.

The only special temptation that had tried me during my captivity was the temptation to be anxious as to how my parents would stand the strain. They were both over eighty and my mother was delicate. "Your old mother will fall down dead when she hears this," the well known voice I had learned to recognize as belonging to the enemy kept telling me insistently. "Be anxious for *nothing*," was as continually, quietly and steadily brought to mind. "I will obey Thy word, Lord, and not be anxious about them." And the Lord took care of them—of course.

One day the newspaper at home in Bergen said that a young missionary, a Miss Monsen, had been captured by pirates in China. My youngest sister, who saw it first, hurried home to tell my parents before they read the paper. When she told them about the young missionary, my Mother said: "That is hard for a young missionary, it would have been better if it had been our Marie; she has been so long in China and knows the people."

When Mother was told that it was her daughter who had been captured, she said: "It is a good thing it isn't a young missionary." She did not fall down dead, she lived for twelve years after that.

A whole week before my release, a cable telling of my being free reached Norway and several other countries. This came about in the following way. The Norwegian, American and British consuls had kept the Governor of Shantung alive to his responsibility for my release by persistent reminders. The Governor wearied of their insistence, and decided that the simplest way to be left in peace was to send out a radio message saying that I was free.

Praise meetings for my deliverance were held at home in Norway and in other countries too, while I was still being held captive and had the most difficult days of all ahead of me. Those praise meetings had a wonderful power to bless the prisoner out in China. I was filled with an inexplicable and quite overwhelming joy those days. My heart sang within me. I could do no other than thank and praise

God all day long, though those were the most trying days, when the pirates were laying their plans for carrying me off.

I had to share this joy with someone, so I took out pen and paper and half hidden behind a coat I had hung up, a whole pile of praise letters were written. The Second Mate's old straw hat, hanging on a wooden peg was my temporary letter-box.

Long after, a Swedish missionary told me that two people in Sweden, who did not know me personally, were awakened in the middle of the night, greatly burdened about me and had prayed for me just at the time when I was taken captive, before anyone had any idea of my circumstances.

The letter quoted below was written on the seventh day to friends in Denmark, who kept it faithfully and lent it to me when they heard I was writing this account now.

"Safe in the arms of Jesus"
Where are we? 26 April 1929.

Dear—

In Tientsin twenty (?) bandits came on board. They have now held the ship for six days. They say they are going today, but they do not appear to be in any hurry about it. I have seen much devilry these days. All the other passengers were thrown out of their cabins; I have been allowed to keep mine. Have been alone with them up here on deck.

I have been delivered from all fear. God keeps His promises. The God of the promises is a living God and He has hidden me in the secret of His presence from all their strife of tongues.

The question of my being carried away has been under discussion, but "The blood of the Lamb is sprinkled on my doorposts," and the destroyer must pass by. The poor passengers, two hundred of them, are the prisoners of the pirates. I am the Lord's prisoner. How different my circumstances are from theirs!

Confusion and violence reigned for five days and nights. Last night they were probably tired themselves and went to sleep, so I had a lovely night, slept like a log.

I am lying behind a rug writing this. It is hardest for those who were expecting me and for the C.I.M. friends in Tientsin, because they know by now that I have disappeared, but the Lord will see them through their anxiety just as He is seeing me through. I am walking along higher paths now, and I thank God for this experience. It will work together for my good and for the good of many. Jesus is the Conqueror and He is with me all the days. The victory that overcomes the world is our faith.

With loving greetings to you all, from the prisoner of Jesus Christ,

Marie

· · · · ·

"God is our refuge and strength, a very present help in trouble" (Psalms 46:1).

Also from Kingsley Press

THE AWAKENING

By Marie Monsen

REVIVAL! It was a long time coming. For twenty long years Marie Monsen prayed for revival in China. She had heard reports of how God's Spirit was being poured out in abundance in other countries, particularly in nearby Korea; so she began praying for funds to be able to travel there in order to bring back some of the glowing coals to her own mission field. But that was not God's way. The still, small voice of God seemed to whisper, "What is happening in Korea can happen in China if you will pay the price in prayer." Marie Monsen took up the challenge and gave her solemn promise: "Then I will pray until I receive."

The Awakening is Miss Monsen's own vivid account of the revival that came in answer to prayer. Leslie Lyall calls her the "pioneer" of the revival movement—the handmaiden upon whom the Spirit was first poured out. He writes: "Her surgical skill in exposing the sins hidden within the Church and lurking behind the smiling exterior of many a trusted Christian—even many a trusted Christian leader—and her quiet insistence on a clear-cut experience of the new birth set the pattern for others to follow."

The emphasis in these pages is on the place given to prayer both before and during the revival, as well as on the necessity of self-emptying, confession, and repentance in order to make way for the infilling of the Spirit.

One of the best ways to stir ourselves up to pray for revival in our own generation is to read the accounts of past awakenings, such as those found in the pages of this book. Surely God is looking for those in every generation who will solemnly take up the challenge and say, with Marie Monsen, "I will pray until I receive."

Buy online at our website: **www.KingsleyPress.com**
Also available as an eBook for Kindle, Nook and iBooks.

An Ordered Life

An Autobiography by G. H. Lang

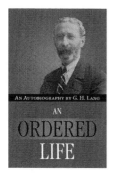

G. H. Lang was a remarkable Bible teacher, preacher and writer of a past generation who should not be forgotten by today's Christians. He inherited the spiritual "mantle" of such giants in the faith as George Müller, Anthony Norris Groves and other notable saints among the early Brethren movement. He traveled all over the world with no fixed means of support other than prayer and faith and no church or other organization to depend on. Like Mr. Müller before him, he told his needs to no one but God. Many times his faith was tried to the limit, as funds for the next part of his journey arrived only at the last minute and from unexpected sources.

This autobiography traces in precise detail the dealings of God with his soul, from the day of his conversion at the tender age of seven, through the twilight years when bodily infirmity restricted most of his former activities. You will be amazed, as you read these pages, to see how quickly and continually a soul can grow in grace and in the knowledge of spiritual things if they will wholly follow the Lord.

Horace Bushnell once wrote that every man's life is a plan of God, and that it's our duty as human beings to find and follow that plan. As Mr. Lang looks back over his long and varied life in the pages of this book, he frequently points out the many times God prepared him in the present for some future work or role. Spiritual life applications abound throughout the book, making it not just a life story but a spiritual training manual of sorts. Preachers will find sermon starters and illustrations in every chapter. Readers of all kinds will benefit from this close-up view of the dealings of God with the soul of one who made it his life's business to follow the Lamb wherever He should lead.

Buy online at our website: **www.KingsleyPress.com**
Also available for Kindle and iBooks (see Amazon's Kindle Store and Apple's iBookstore for details).

GIPSY SMITH
HIS LIFE AND WORK

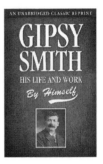

This autobiography of Gipsy Smith (1860-1947) tells the fascinating story of how God's amazing grace reached down into the life of a poor, uneducated gipsy boy and sent him singing and preaching all over Britain and America until he became a household name in many parts and influenced the lives of millions for Christ. He was born and raised in a gipsy tent to parents who made a living selling baskets, tinware and clothes pegs. His father was in and out of jail for various offences, but was gloriously converted during an evangelistic meeting. His mother died when he was only five years old.

Converted at the age of sixteen, Gipsy taught himself to read and write and began to practice preaching. His beautiful singing voice earned him the nickname "the singing gipsy boy," as he sang hymns to the people he met. At age seventeen he became an evangelist with the Christian Mission (which became the Salvation Army) and began to attract large crowds. Leaving the Salvation Army in 1882, he became an itinerant evangelist working with a variety of organizations. It is said that he never had a meeting without conversions. He was a born orator. One of the Boston papers described him as "the greatest of his kind on earth, a spiritual phenomenon, an intellectual prodigy and a musical and oratorical paragon."

His autobiography is full of anedotes and stories from his preaching experiences in many different places. It's a book you won't want to put down until you're finished!

Buy online at our website: **www.KingsleyPress.com**
Also available as an eBook for Kindle, Nook and iBooks.